Journey to My Father, ISAAC BASHEVIS SINGER

Journey to My Father, Isaac Bashevis Singer

Israel Zamir

Translated from the Hebrew
by Barbara Harshav

ARCADE PUBLISHING · NEW YORK

FIRST ENGLISH-LANGUAGE EDITION

Excerpts from "From the Old and New House" by Isaac Bashevis Singer reprinted from *The Jewish Daily Forward*. Used by permission.

Excerpts from *Nobel Lecture* by Isaac Bashevis Singer copyright © 1978 by the Nobel Foundation. Reprinted by permission of Farrar, Straus & Giroux, Inc.

Library of Congress Cataloging-in-Publication Data

Zamir, Israel, 1929–
    [Avi, Yitshak Bashevis-Zinger. English]
    Journey to my father, Isaac Bashevis Singer / Israel Zamir ; translated from the Hebrew by Barbara Harshav. —1st English-language ed.
        p.   cm.
    ISBN 1-55970-309-1
    1. Singer, Isaac Bashevis, 1904–1991—Biography. 2. Authors, Yiddish—United States—Biography. 3. Zamir, Israel, 1929– —Biography. 4. Authors, Israeli—Biography. 5. Fathers and sons— Biography. I. Harshav, Barbara, 1940– . II. Title.
PJ5129.S49Z9613   1995
839'.0933—dc20   95-17860

Published in the United States by Arcade Publishing, Inc., New York

Distributed by Little, Brown and Company

10 9 8 7 6 5 4 3 2 1

BP

PRINTED IN THE UNITED STATES OF AMERICA

CONTENTS

PREFACE

I went on a journey to my father, in a quest for his life and works. I learned later that my father shared the same wish; he too was looking to find his son, and we found ourselves traveling together on the same journey. A generation separated us. He had left Warsaw in 1935 when I was five years old, and we met again in New York twenty years later. From that moment on, each of us tried to bridge the gap of time.

The journey ended with his death in July 1991. I stood at his fresh grave, feeling I had missed so much because I hadn't known him better; and memories surfaced. Throughout the years, in the course of our fragmented and short times together, I had taken ample notes. Back in Israel after the funeral, feeling confused and sad, I returned to my notes and felt compelled to write more. Hoping, no doubt, that in so doing I would perhaps understand my father better and in a way bring him back to me. This is neither a biography of my father nor an evaluation of his literary work. That has been done by others more qualified than me. This is, rather, a personal account of what started as a failed father-son relationship and ended in a mature friendship.

When I was in my mid-twenties, I met my father for the first time after twenty years and spent several years in New York as an official representative of my kibbutz's youth movement. My father and I saw each other a great deal and continued to keep up, later, when he visited me in Israel. Despite a slow start, our relationship evolved into something that could be called a solid bond, reaching a semblance of family ties. As I grew closer to my father, I discovered all his books, most of which I ended up translating into Hebrew. We collaborated on every story I translated. It was primarily through these work sessions — with my father sitting next to me and me asking him questions for translation purposes — that I got to know him better. Each of my translation queries seemed to trigger memories of his childhood, my childhood, and other periods in our lives. Through these long explorations of his past, the twenty-year gap between us slowly narrowed.

In 1978, when my father won the Nobel Prize for literature, he invited me to accompany him to Stockholm and share that momentous and exciting event. Later, during the course of one of my visits to New York in the 1980s, I remember reading to my father two passages from his collection of stories called *A Friend of Kafka*, which included the story "The Son." The two passages describe the protagonist waiting for his son at the port of New York after not seeing him for twenty years. As he waited, the thought went through his mind, "After all, what is a son? How is my seed closer to me than anybody else's? What is the value of the closeness of flesh and blood? Aren't we all the foam of one general biological shot?" And in another place: "He [the son] doesn't fit in my house now or in my conditions outside my house. I don't have a room for him or a bed or money or time."

"Do you still feel like that about your son?" I asked him, amused.

He smiled and waved off the question. After a long pause, he finally said, "Those were philosophical thoughts meant to hide my excitement and fear of meeting you. I had every reason in the world to worry about that meeting. I had no desire to apologize to you for leaving your mother. I knew very little about you, but from the little I did know, I understood that you had socialist tendencies. That was in the middle of the 1950s, the age of McCarthyism in America, and I was scared I'd be thrown out of this country because of you. And it's true, I didn't have a room for you at that time, or a bed, or money, or time."

"So why did you invite me to New York? What was the logic behind the invitation?" I wondered.

He stared at me, frowned, and almost yelled, "Logic? Since when does logic dictate the lives of the Jews? Did you ever hear of a people that was exiled from its country, wandered in exile for two thousand years, and didn't assimilate? Most exiles assimilate into their new environment after one or two generations. Millions of Italians who immigrated to this country are now considered 'real Americans.' By the second or third generation they don't speak Italian anymore. But the Jews, after two thousand years of exile, kept Hebrew, Aramaic, and Yiddish. Their culture wandered with them from one country to another. They didn't abandon their faith, and after two thousand years they returned to the land of Israel. Do you find logic here? This is the only case in human history where a people was preserved and didn't assimilate. Not one theory can explain the secret of the Jewish people's survival. My son, the world has never ever been run according to logic. If you're here, in New York, you were meant to come here, despite all the hesitations. And you *had* to translate my works into Hebrew."

"Soon you'll interpret my coming to you as a command of 'higher forces,' connected with demons and ghosts," I said.

"What makes you think it's not?" he replied, with the familiar twinkle in his eyes.

Journey to My Father, Isaac Bashevis Singer

1

ON THE WAY TO BETH-EL

July 24, 1991, was one of those outrageously hot, dusty days we Israelis call a *Sharav*. Secretary of State James Baker was in Jerusalem to discuss the composition of the Palestinian delegation to the peace talks with the Israeli prime minister. That evening, I worked on an editorial until midnight, unaware that, twenty-four hours later, I would be on my way to New York, to my father's funeral.

At four in the morning my phone rang. Half asleep, I picked it up, expecting to hear the night editor on the line. But it was my daughter Merav, calling from San Francisco where she was studying. Alma, my father's wife, had just informed her of his death. Even though I had known that his condition was critical, the news stunned me. I lay awake for a long time, trying to register the news. Despite the missing twenty years from childhood to adulthood when I hadn't seen him, I had nevertheless managed to "build" a father for myself. Instead of the love that develops from childhood on, there was friendship and companionship between us. Now he was dead. He had never wanted to talk about death and kept putting it off. Did he think it wouldn't happen to him? I loved his works. I read his books over and over and translated many of them into Hebrew. Translating probably expressed my desire to connect with my father, get to know him, understand him.

My father had hovered between life and death for a long time. Alma had told me that he had recently suffered a few heart attacks and had spent many weeks in Saint Francis Hospital in Miami. His last days were in the Douglas Gardens Rest Home, where he died. One examination had revealed liver cancer. He had apparently been taking radiation treatments that intensified his suffering. According to Alma, the radiation hurt more than it helped. From time to time, he would come to with an awful groan of pain. "His eyes would open wide and he looked like a little boy, pleading for help; and I couldn't do a thing to save him. That look will always haunt me," she said.

At eight in the morning, Israeli radio announced my father's death. From then on, writers and intellectuals from around the world were asked to assess his literary contribution. Our plane took off late; it was almost midnight. As I was flying to New York for what would be my last visit to my father, I tried sorting out our fragmented and disconnected past. Though I had spent most of my life far away from him, each visit had brought us closer. Bits of unrelated stories about his youth in Poland came back to me. And I remembered the story my father had told me of his visit to one of his lady friends who lived in a garret in Warsaw. As they lay in bed, there was a knock on the door. The husband appeared on the threshold, and the lover — my father — dashed out through the window to the roof, where he stood naked and freezing, hopelessly waiting for his mistress to toss his clothes to him. My father told me that tale long before it appeared in one of his stories. His ability to charm women was legendary. Alma knew and accepted his weaknesses. She often said that "to live with a great artist means living with greatness accompanied by weakness. But the spiritual and personal

wealth that Isaac gave me went beyond all my expectations."
She knew that, in the end, he would always come back to her.

A flight attendant went by, handing out blankets. A young
woman sat next to me, reading a book. I glanced at her and was
reminded of one of my father's books, *The Penitent*. The protagonist, Joseph Shapiro, was fleeing from some sin he had
committed. But while engaged in conversation with a woman
next to him on a plane, he couldn't overcome his lust for her
and sinned again.

The memories wouldn't let go of me. I was reliving my first
meeting with my father, along with the tension I had felt at the
port of New York in 1955. After twenty years of silence, our
mutual anxiety had been intense. And my coming to live in his
New York apartment proved very difficult for both of us in the
beginning. I was also reliving our constant arguments, starting
from that first encounter.

The lights came on in the plane. The night was over. The
flight attendant distributed newspapers. "The president of the
Soviet Union and secretary of the Communist party Mikhail
Gorbachev proposes a new platform for his party and rejects
some theories of Marxism-Leninism." I was reminded of one of
many bitter arguments I had had with my father over Stalin,
"savior of the people," about a week into my first visit. He kept
arguing that the Soviet regime was corrupt, nothing but "base
instincts and demoralization, whose disgrace would be revealed
publicly." His words had offended me, and I called him a
reactionary. He was right, it turned out. The world had refused
to believe the facts in the newspapers. During the course of that
first visit, he suggested that I translate his works into Hebrew,
but I ignored the idea. Sitting at a desk didn't appeal to me. I
wanted to be a productive man. Like most Israelis from a kibbutz, I wanted to live by the sweat of my brow, a pioneer

bringing bread out of the earth, and not be a luftmensch like my father. But after reading his stories I was won over and was pleased to take on the task of translating most of his work into Hebrew.

After landing in Brussels for refueling, I got off the plane to stretch my legs and walked up and down the passenger terminal for about two hours. That, again, reminded me of the way my father used to walk daily around the streets of New York. He would sometimes cover four or five kilometers on his walks.

We took off again and were immediately enveloped in white, thick clouds, as in a featherbed. The plane began swaying, and the captain asked us to fasten our seat belts. How absurd it would be, I thought, to crash on the way to my father's funeral.

And how did they conduct funerals in America? I was curious. I remembered seeing processions of cars with their headlights on, driving to the cemetery. Thousands of Singer admirers would no doubt attend my father's funeral. They would have to close off a special lane to avoid blocking traffic. Should I say kaddish for my father, I wondered? I didn't even have a yarmulke with me. I closed my eyes, and my father's face appeared in my mind's eye.

"You want me to say kaddish at your grave?"

My father smiled and shook his head. I knew he didn't believe in the formal practices of religion. But on second thought, he replied: "Gigi, what do you think about saying kaddish after all? It'll be my small revenge to see my socialist son in a yarmulke."

"I think I'll write a brief eulogy," I added. "You object?"

"Whatever you want. But don't praise me too much. I should have written my own eulogy. I'm worried about what those schlemiels down there are going to say about me."

The plane landed in New York.

On Sunday, my wife and I went to the funeral parlor on Riverside Drive in Manhattan. There were already a great many people there. According to the newspapers, about three hundred people attended — intellectuals, friends, neighbors, and Yiddishists. The hall filled very quickly. Rabbi Berkowitz, my father's close friend, delivered the eulogy, in which he managed to intersperse a good deal of humor. One of the anecdotes he told was about my father's being asked why *Gimpel the Fool* had achieved such commercial success. He replied that he was convinced that many of the readers thought the book was about Gimbel's department store, which had recently closed. "I think I'll call my next collection of stories *Macy's the Idiot*." Berkowitz went on to talk about Stockholm and the Nobel ceremonies he had attended as part of my father's entourage. In the middle of his eulogy, the microphone began chirping and beeping. None of the staff of the funeral home seemed to be on hand, and the helpless rabbi, looking skyward, explained the static as the interventions of the demons and ghosts of my father's heroes, who were manifesting their mourning.

I was asked to speak after Rabbi Berkowitz. A bit shaky, I climbed the platform and delivered my eulogy:

> If I had asked my father what he wanted me to say about him when he departed this world, he would probably have smiled, trained his blue eyes on me, and replied: "Son, don't say anything; but if you insist, it'd be better if you told a story. People love stories."
>
> So, in your honor, father, I shall tell a story:
>
> One day, we were taking a walk along Broadway, and my father, as usual, was scattering seeds for the

pigeons. Suddenly a policeman came up to us and said: "Sir, it's against the law to litter the street."

My father looked at him, somewhat frightened, and answered: "Mr. Policeman, it's winter now, it's cold. Hungry pigeons huddle on roofs open to the wind, hoping somebody will take pity on them and feed them. Who knows, maybe in the next incarnation, the two of us will come back as hungry pigeons."

The policeman looked at us. He clearly had never heard such an excuse: "But sir, it's against the law," he said.

We left.

The next day we came back. My father looked around and didn't see any policeman. When the sack of seeds was empty, the policeman from the previous day burst out of a bar, rushed up to my father, and, pulling out a book from his coat pocket, asked: "Mr. Singer, can you sign your book *Old Love* for me?"

Surprised and pleased, my father quickly signed his book. "If a New York policeman asks a Yiddish writer to sign his book, there's still hope," he remarked after the policeman left. That day my father was as happy as if he had received a precious gift.

Thank you, father, for being with us in this world. Your writings have enriched our lives and made them more human. And maybe even more Jewish.

I assumed that when the ceremony was over, a convoy of cars would line up to go to the cemetery. Much to my surprise, however, everyone quickly said good-bye and left. Alma had ordered a limousine, but there was not enough room in it for

her family, myself, and my wife Aviva to go together. I
shouldn't bother coming to the burial, she said, but I insisted,
and one of my friends drove us in his car. It seemed a long trip,
and when we finally reached Beth-El Cemetery in New Jersey,
we had a lot of trouble finding the grave. When we arrived, the
coffin had already been lowered into the ground, and the family
members were requested to cover it with earth. We picked up
shovels and started filling in the grave. I cautiously asked Alma if
I should say kaddish, and she replied with a shrug that meant,
whatever you want. There was an uneasy silence, someone
handed me a yarmulke, and I said kaddish. A man from the
funeral parlor began reciting an abbreviated version of the
traditional prayer at the grave, "God Full of Mercy," and everything quickly came to an end. There weren't even the customary ten men required for a prayer minyan.

Had the funeral taken place in Israel, thousands would have
attended. Alma didn't grant my plea to bury my father in Israel.
It would cost too much, she said. And I was very sorry about it.
In Israel, Singer's grave would have become a pilgrimage site for
Yiddishists, intellectuals, tourists of all kinds. But this godforsaken place would attract no one. There would never be anyone
to pay homage to my father in New Jersey. It left me doubly sad.

I was reminded of the Yiddish poet Itsik Manger, who, as he
embarked on a trip abroad, told a journalist friend of mine: "If I
should die in America, bring me back to Israel! In New York,
not even a dog will come to my funeral."

As the limousine was about to leave the cemetery, the electronic gate wouldn't open. Our two cars stopped. The manager
came out of his office and matter-of-factly informed Alma that
the money for the plot hadn't been paid in full, and according to
instructions, no one was allowed to leave the cemetery until it
was paid. Alma tried explaining to him who had been buried. It

made no impression on the manager, who said: "Lady, we got a crew here and we got to take care of paying them." Alma pulled out her checkbook and paid.

Turning back, I gave a last look at my father's grave. The circle was now closed. Isaac Bashevis Singer, the writer, the Nobel laureate, rests somewhere in a remote land, where no one, or only very few people, will ever visit his grave.

That was my last chapter with my father.

2

THE FIRST ENCOUNTER

A flock of gray seagulls over the bow of the ship heralded the American shore. The travelers, who had formed one solid group during the long trip, slowly began peeling off, each with his own bags. Thick fog closed in all around, visibility shrank, and we suddenly found ourselves swaddled in a thick, white, cold featherbed. The ship slowed down, groping its way like a blind man, swaying drunkenly from side to side. Loud bells rang a warning to stray ships in the dense fog. The loudspeaker was broadcasting urgent orders to the crew. Ropes were being stretched, hooks attached, and the crew was removing anything that might be washed overboard. Thunder echoed dully, and the passengers were ordered to go below. Anxiety had tightened my stomach. I felt some pain.

I was left alone in the stern, my eyes fixed on the foamy wake. A strong wind was blowing. I gripped the rail and thought of my father. The journey had come to an end. I was over-whelmed, knowing that on this day in February 1955 we were going to come face-to-face, father and son, for the first time after twenty years. My father. What kind of paternal feelings could a father express toward his twenty-five-year-old son? Did we have anything in common after all this time?

"Father!" I roared, my voice covering the howling wind. An enormous wave flooded the deck. I grew suddenly dizzy and got sick to my stomach. My eyes were salty and burning. Wet, worn-out, empty, hanging on to the railing, I ran to my cabin to wash up before we docked.

When I was five years old, we had parted ways. My father sailed for America. My mother and I, after some peregrination, finally made it to Palestine. For a few years, all communication was cut off. Then he would write from time to time. He wanted to know how I was doing, who my friends were, and once he even asked "if I had young ladies." He felt the need to get close and was offended by my reluctance to communicate back. His Hebrew was strange, a blend of Talmudic and nineteenth-century Haskalah Hebrew. I was ashamed of the way he put his words together, and I destroyed his letters. Sometimes at Rosh Hashanah or on my birthday, he would send a few dollars. Did he feel paternal, or was it guilt? I took the money — in those days I needed pocket money — but I didn't feel any affection for him. Over the years, I managed to put him out of my mind and thought of my father only rarely. Although I got used to the notion that he existed somewhere, as I got used to my own breathing, it remained for many years an abstract notion nonetheless.

When I heard my name on the ship's loudspeaker, I hurried to the immigration official, who asked sternly: "Who are you going to?"

"My father," I said innocently.

He looked at me with surprise and continued asking questions. Without realizing, I was discussing my personal affairs with him.

"How long since you've seen him?"

"Twenty years."

"Oh." He blinked. His expression softened and he glanced at me. He was no doubt imagining an emotional encounter between father and son.

"How many years do you want to stay in our country?"

"Three months."

"Not longer?" he asked, in the tones of a betrayed father.

"No. I promised a girl I'd come back the day she gets out of the army."

"I'll give you an extension of one year. We don't like to be hard on our guests." He shook my hand and wished me good luck. Another official suspiciously examined my customs declaration, which was empty. I didn't have anything to declare. I owned one suit, bought for me by the storekeeper at the kibbutz, and I had a few gifts that some of the members were sending to their relatives.

During the trip, I wanted to buy my father a present, but I had no idea what. I went to the gift shop on the ship and asked for help. The saleswoman wanted to know how old my father was and how big his feet were. Again, I had no idea. She pulled out a little sack of dirt with a picture of the Matriarch Rachel on it. The look in my eyes told her that it was a mistake. Then she took a flat brass plate off the wall; it was engraved with a picture of a Yemenite girl carrying a pitcher on her head. I ended up buying a small ashtray.

I pictured this father I had not seen in twenty years as one of those thick-necked American tourists who would swoop down on the kibbutz in a fancy car, showing their potbellies in cotton pants, sporting cameras and cigars. They'd stay a little while, admire everything in a loud voice, smile roguishly, and go away as they had come, in a cloud of dust. If that's how my father was, I thought sadly, the ashtray certainly wouldn't do.

The ship was fourteen hours late. We were supposed to dock

at eight in the morning, but because of the heavy fog, we didn't get into port until ten at night. From the distance, skyscrapers flickered their thousands of lights. The rain didn't let up. Thin sprays were caught in the light beams. It was pitch-dark by the time we got off the ship.

When my turn came to disembark, I straightened my collar, smoothed my hair, and stepped onto the gangplank. As I descended I heard Hasidic singing. For a moment I was surprised. Could he be one of them? But since when had he been Hasidic? Why hadn't he written to us about it? My gullet rose and fell in embarrassment. Looking back, I saw a couple of yeshiva students dressed in silk, with curly earlocks, calmly singing and waving their arms behind me. I imagined that they were probably celebrating the great privilege of making a pilgrimage to the holy community of New York, and basking in the shadow of the Lubavitcher rebbe.

I was finally off the ship. I looked around. No one had come to greet me. An official pointed to show us where to go. Customs was teeming. Officials in splendid uniforms with knowing eyes were carefully rummaging through suitcases. When the baggage inspection was over, the other travelers fell into the arms of those who had come to welcome them. I stood there confused. In front of me, a young couple was kissing passionately, making up for lost time. They looked at each other in disbelief, jostled me, and went on their way. Restored joy. I trudged helplessly to the end of the hall, hoping to find my father near my bags, but a large Yemenite family, crowded around their patriarch who had arrived on the ship, prevented me from moving farther. Children and grandchildren were surrounding him in a tight circle, speaking excitedly all at the same time. They were making desperate gestures in an effort to describe the new world to him. The grandfather nodded, wiping his tears. From time to time, he squinted at one of his offspring with a mixture of surprise and emotion. It was clear that for him, they had already lost the charm of the East, with their big bellies, good suits, starched shirts, and colorful bow ties. I could feel the abyss separating the old man of the Yemenite neighborhood in Tel Aviv from his "American" family; he had made his way to Israel by donkey or camel. His children or grandchildren had been born in Brooklyn.

The clock at the port read 2:00 A.M. The customs officials changed shifts.

"Why don't you go to Information and ask them to page your father?" a woman suggested. I rejected that idea. I was too nervous. I wanted to meet him quietly. The customs hall emptied out. It then occurred to me that he might have gotten sick and couldn't come. I closed myself in a phone booth and called his home. His wife Alma answered.

"Hello, this is the son. Is your husband home?"

"No," she replied, excited. "I'm glad you arrived. My husband left home at seven this morning and has been at the port all day looking for you."

"Here?"

"Oh my God, what happened to him?"

I calmed her down and assured her that we'd find each other. I continued examining those left at the dock more carefully.

A fair-skinned man who was running around drew my attention. He stood in the entrance, facing the ship, chomping nervously on a cigar. I glanced at him furtively, looking for something we might have in common. He was medium height, with reddish hair, and had a round face and a mysterious smile on his lips. He turned to me for a moment and winked mischievously, like a partner in crime. He had bold, steel-blue eyes and seemed to fit my father's description. That's him! No doubt about it! I felt my heart pounding. Mustering up my courage, I approached him.

"Might you be Mr. Singer?"

"I might," he replied, imitating my singsong voice.

"Is it possible that you're my father?" I added in the same tone. I was worried that my voice would fail me.

He grew serious all at once and stared at me a long time. His pupils darted around like a pair of moths at a light. He finally murmured, half to me, half to himself: "It's possible, anything's possible. You never know if your pranks from bygone times didn't produce a son who'll pop up suddenly from across the ocean and demand his share of the inheritance."

Showing my irritation, I left him promptly. The customs official hurried me out. I picked up my suitcase and left. A cold wind assaulted me with such force that I almost stumbled. The streets were dark and deserted. Huge raindrops poured down in crooked streams. New York looked very ugly. There were many people crowded around a barricade near the gate of the port, waiting to welcome relatives. As I approached them, I identified my father. This time it felt right; I knew it was him. He was standing off to the side of the street and looking at me closely, restrained. That had to be the way he looked, I was sure; this man's medium height and light-skinned face seemed to fit what I thought corresponded to my father's features. His short chin ended in a tiny knob; his eyeglasses, even the coat and felt hat he wore, seemed right to me. Not allowing myself to show my excitement, I tried to look calm and slowly passed him by.

"Gigi?" the man called out. I hadn't heard my childhood name in so many years!

"Yes," I responded quickly, like a soldier in basic training. We shook hands. He kissed me. We stood there, embarrassed and silent. All my life, I had imagined this encounter with my father. There we both were, and I was choked up and exhausted, unable to say a thing. We stood in silence for a long while until he decided to hail a cab. I felt as though I was coming out of a deep sleep.

"I'll help you carry your suitcase," he said.

I glanced at him, assessing his strength. He looked thin and fragile.

"I can handle it," I answered.

I sensed at once that I had offended him, because he fell silent. A blinding flash of light revealed gray clouds scurrying across the sky, illuminating the horizon for a moment. Then came the thunder. The door of a bar across the street opened, and two waiters tossed a drunk into a puddle; he landed with a splash in the water, moaning and groaning. New York.

The taxi rushed forward. Squares of light from nightclubs focused for a second, lighting up my father's face. His skull was round and shining, his hair brown and thin.

"How was the crossing?"

"Stormy."

"Why were you the last one out?"

"I was looking for you."

"I see. How's Mother?"

"What's that supposed to mean?"

He fell silent again. He continued asking me questions about my girlfriend. I ignored him and didn't answer. He respected my silence. But the silence was oppressive. A cold sweat began creeping over my body, the start of an old feeling. A familiar and unbearable tension took hold of me. I hunched over and clung to the window. The chilled glass cooled my hot forehead. Everything seemed so strange to me. I knew that I ought to break this insufferable silence, knock down the wall with some healing speech, but I was paralyzed. A rainbow of dazzling lights indicated that Broadway was close by. From the somber docks, New York was changing its image, showing its playful side. I didn't feel comfortable in that bright light. I felt exposed, and I didn't want my father to see what was going on inside of me. It was so difficult for me to be here in New York, sitting next to this stranger, my father. I had trouble remembering the dark, heavy nights of the Negev. It had vanished so quickly. Just a little while before I had been an integral part of a group of fighters who had made their home in an Arabic grove in the Negev. Night after night we raided the enemy's fortifications. Before dawn we'd return, torn, frozen, carrying stretchers. Our casualties seemed to follow the order of our cots in the grove. We'd count how many nights before our long furlough.

One day we carried Dudik, the guy in the cot next to mine. His belly was torn to shreds. I was afraid that my final moment had come too. All the way, as we were carrying Dudik, I thought of my girlfriend, of Mother, of the father in America I had never known. I was shamelessly composing my own eulogy. The night was so clear and so bright. We stole to the foot of the fortified hill, crawling to our firing positions, waiting tensely for the order to attack. We lay perfectly still. The frost was ruthless. I was shivering with cold on the one hand and sweating with fear on the other. A tracer bullet passed slowly across the horizon. In the distance, the lights of Gaza flickered. From time to time, isolated spears of searchlight stabbed the night. I no longer felt my body; the cold was destroying me completely. I felt physically dead and waited for the bullet to carry out its assigned mission. I even thought with some sympathy of my fellow soldiers, and the weight they'd have to load on their backs!

Drink.

I pulled out the cork. My mouth clung feverishly to the

bottle, and the liquid began a dance of death in my belly. My guts were on fire.

The static on the wireless suddenly stopped. This was it. We waited for the familiar three beeps that would signal "Attack!" I tensed my muscles; my finger moved over the safety catch. I was ready for the final attack on my lost hopes. The beeps were delayed. The silence of the wireless was replaced by the slow, calm whisper of the commander: "Return, return. I repeat. Return. Over." A cease-fire was signed that night in Rhodes. Was that the hand of fate? Or had I gotten my life back as a birthday present? I was twenty years old that day. What if the signing had been delayed by a day? Would I now be in New York, or under a pile of earth like my buddies in the unit? Those questions filled my mind as I sat next to my father in the cab taking us to his home.

The cab made its way along Central Park West. Splendid, calm buildings rose up. A cold wind blew from the north. The avenue shook its head and buried its feet in a blanket of rusty autumn leaves. My father gazed at me a long time, trying to figure out what was going on within me. His eyes were wide open, full, velvety soft.

"Son, there are no accidents in this world. If you're alive, it means you had to stay alive."

Was he reading my mind? Fatherhood was probably strong enough to knock down a twenty-year wall with one swipe, I was convinced.

It occurred to me that he too had no doubt been thinking of the passage of time, of his own life, the bundle that had come undone, the son and wife he had left behind in Poland. Maybe he had even imagined the adventures they had gone through, cut off from him: their trek to Russia, their escape to Turkey in the late thirties, their desolate lives in cheap hotels in Istanbul, without passports, without money in their pockets, their terror at every policeman, every knock on the door. He didn't send money. He said he didn't have any. Then came the war, and they vanished from his life. He later said that he had had visions, and in his dreams he saw his son in a convoy making its way to Auschwitz. He would wake up horrified, with a prayer on his lips.

If we were meeting again — a father and son who had never been close — that was simply the will of Providence. The life I'd saved from the war was one he didn't know at all. But at that moment in the taxi, I was convinced that he had drawn it out of me, not out of himself. And at that instant, I believed that blood ties didn't lie. And perhaps it was that belief that helped me slowly push aside some walls between us.

3

WE GROW CLOSE FOR A MOMENT

We arrived at my father's New York home. The living room was lined with books, and there were newspapers all over the coffee table. In the middle of the living room was a folding bed bought especially for me, I was told. Alma gave me a friendly welcome. "Gigi, I'm very glad you came. We'll talk later," she said. "Your father's very tired. He's been waiting for you at the port since early morning. He'd better go to sleep now. I've got to get up early for work tomorrow." We all went to bed.

The next day, I woke up early and looked out their fourteenth-floor window. I had never been in such a high building. Beneath me I saw a park full of green trees — Central Park — and was struck by the difference of landscape. In Israel there is no such dark, fresh greenery. Mount Gilboa is yellow most of the year. I was fascinated by this new scenery and by the street with cars zooming by. "So you're finally in America," I said to myself. I was curious to explore New York. I was also puzzled by the fact that I didn't feel anything for my father.

All my life I had dreamed of meeting him. I imagined that it would be very emotional, that we'd fall crying into each other's arms. And now that we were finally together, my heart was empty and dry. My absence of feelings for my father upset me.

A while later my father woke up and, wrapped in a robe, crossed the room and went to the bathroom. I noticed his legs; they were thin and very white. Unlike me, he had never had to work in the field, I told myself. Still wearing his bathrobe, he hurried to his armchair and started writing, oblivious of my being there. He never greeted me, not a word. Embarrassed, not knowing what to do, I stared out the window, stealing a glance at him every now and then. That morning I was seeing him for the first time in daylight. I could see a resemblance between us. The same structure of the face, the fair coloring, the blue eyes, the mouth, the nose; but his ears stuck out so much! I watched him glance furtively at me, and our eyes would meet from time to time. We were both embarrassed and remained silent. Assuming that it was the host's duty to take care of his guest, I decided that it wasn't up to me to start a conversation. He stopped writing and raised his eyebrows, staring at me with an expression of disbelief, at this son who seemed to have suddenly popped up out of nowhere and sat smiling at him. He was perhaps overwhelmed, I told myself, and didn't know what to say to his newfound son. He was no doubt hiding his awkwardness in his papers. Or was it that picking me up and bringing me to his home was all that I could expect of him? I was puzzled. Alma had gotten up early and gone to work. I had no idea how to communicate with him. What language was I supposed to speak? Hebrew? Yiddish? English? My Yiddish was terrible; my English was shaky. And if his letters were any indication, his Hebrew was the language of the Eastern European Ashkenazi synagogue, not of modern Israel, and one that I had trouble understanding. He seemed to be done writing and stood up, suggesting that we have something to eat.

We went into the kitchen, which was twice the size of my room at the kibbutz, and made ourselves some breakfast. The awkwardness between us continued.

"Well, Gigi, you're in New York now. This is a big metropolis. I'm so glad you've arrived here hale and hearty." His Hebrew reminded me of the obsolete writers of the Haskalah. I replied in my broken English, and he seemed to take offense. Alma later told me that, in anticipation of my arrival, he had been polishing his Hebrew. When he first began writing, he had written in that language, he told me. Now here was his son rejecting his efforts to communicate.

After breakfast, we took a bus across the park and went to the Metropolitan Museum of Art. I was terribly excited as I stood for several minutes in front of paintings by Van Gogh, Cezanne, Rembrandt, Picasso. But my father walked indifferently past them without ever stopping. He kept glancing at his watch, and after twenty minutes, he announced: "Let's go back home. I've got a lot of work to do."

I regretted this brief visit but knew that I couldn't steal his precious working time. As we left the museum, it started raining. And looking at my shoes, my father asked why I wasn't wearing rubbers. I didn't own any, I answered.

"I'll buy you some," my father said. I learned later that, for him, saying was the same as actually doing. He never bought me any rubbers, of course.

We took a bus back to Broadway.

"We'll go have something to eat," he announced. The cafeteria was full. Having just arrived from a country where rationing was in effect, I found myself staring at the shelves filled with all sorts of delicacies. I didn't dare order meat, being concerned that it was too expensive. So I took two bowls of rice — a delicacy I hadn't tasted in a long time. At the kibbutz, we seldom ate rice, and when we did, it was brown rice. I also took soup and bread. My father looked at me with an astonished expression.

"Why so much rice?"

"I haven't eaten white rice in years," I replied.

"And you eat bread with rice?"

"At our kibbutz, you eat everything with bread."

He raised his eyebrows and, staring at me, he asked: "Gigi, how much do you weigh?"

"Seventy kilograms, about a hundred and fifty pounds."

"Too much. I can't understand why you have to carry a whole grocery store around on your body. Isn't it easier to take only what you need from the shelf? You'll have to lose weight fast."

I sheepishly put back one bowl of rice and the portion of bread. At the kibbutz, I told my father, we ate red meat only when we slaughtered a cow for special occasions, or when our stock of poultry and fish was getting low. But most of the time our diet consisted mainly of vegetables and bread.

"We'll go back to Israel together in three weeks. I've already ordered tickets. It will be my first visit to the Holy Land," my father informed me. I was a bit disappointed to have to return so soon. I hadn't yet seen any of the wonders of America, and he was already talking about my return home.

"When you come, I'll show you the places where I fought," I said.

"Don't bother. I'm not interested in touring the country. All the landscapes in the world are here, in my head," and his finger moved over his brow. "I can describe any landscape without seeing it. I plan to see some of my friends from Warsaw there in Israel."

When we arrived at his apartment, he hurried to his writing

chair and, as was now routine, proceeded to ignore me. What was I to do here? Why had I come? Here I was, a twenty-five-year-old who had finished military service, who had been a fighter and a farmer — a person with a role in society — who suddenly found himself in a foreign environment, artificially rendered idle and dependent on a stranger. Had I known my way around New York, I would have stayed in the museum another few hours.

Within a few days it became obvious that my father wouldn't have time for me. I would have to get along on my own. To clear my head, I went for a walk in the park and was delighted by the friendly squirrels who came up to me without any fear. I had never seen these little animals who looked like mice with foxtails. The smell of the hotdogs coming from the vendors made my mouth water, but I remembered that I didn't have a cent in my pocket. I didn't feel that I could ask him for money. What right did I have to ask for money from a man who was a stranger to me?

My father must have felt the same way; in any case, he didn't offer me any pocket money. Maybe he didn't have any. It was clear that I would have to earn some money on my own if I wanted to get around in New York. But how was I going to find work? I didn't know the language and didn't have a work permit. Back at the apartment, I asked my father to help me find some work.

"Gigi, you want to work for three weeks? In America? It's against the law for you to work here. They'll throw us both out." He looked at me for a long time, as if he were considering asking me something that was obviously bothering him. "Are you mad at me for leaving you and your mother and going to America?"

"It was a long time ago. You probably did what you had to."

"Your mother isn't mad at me either?"

"I didn't say that. But what's between the two of you is none of my business."

Before I left for America, my mother had wanted to unload on me the whole bundle of his "vile deeds," as she put it. I refused to listen, arguing that the statute of limitations applied to those crimes.

"I've rebuilt my life," said my mother, "but you've been damaged by his mean behavior to this very day."

"Damaged? How?"

"By constant longings for a father who is a stranger to you, who promised dozens of times to come and never did, who promised hundreds of times to send money and didn't. When you were three years old, you got a bad ear infection. You cried for days. I begged your father to send for a doctor, but he didn't, claiming he didn't have any money. A few days later, when he came home, as he put his coat on a chair, a dozens zlotys fell out of the pockets onto the floor."

I categorically refused to get involved and didn't answer her. I wanted to come to my father with no emotional baggage. My mother never forgave me for not settling her accounts with him.

"Ronya, your mother, wrote me that you were wounded when the Italians bombed Tel Aviv in 1940. Where exactly were you hit and how long were you in the hospital?" asked my father.

"I was never wounded and I wasn't in the hospital. Where did you hear that?"

"Your mother wrote me about it in a letter."

"I don't believe it. I was never wounded."

"You don't believe me?" he asked, insulted.

After rummaging in his desk drawers for a long time, he

extracted a letter in my mother's handwriting and read me a passage from it. I had been wounded, she had written, and was in the hospital. She begged him to send her money urgently, "to save our Gigi." I took the letter from him and, with the little bit of Yiddish I knew, managed to make out what was written. I was extremely annoyed and didn't know what to say. Settling these old accounts seemed unfair and impossible to me.

"Believe me, son, I didn't have a cent at the time. I got to America in 1935 and wandered around for seven years. I was miserably poor. Every day I survived was a miracle. I couldn't have helped you. Do you believe me?"

"I believe you. I hold no grudges. I wrote you that when I asked to come."

"Yes, yes. I know. Your letter moved me very deeply. I'm so glad you came."

"Really?"

"You don't believe me? Well, I'm not much of a family man, but I'll do everything I can to make you feel comfortable in the three weeks you're here with us." He pulled out a dollar bill and gave it to me.

"No thanks," I replied.

I felt great humiliation and wanted to say: Dear father! You invited me here, shouldn't you make sure I live respectably and don't feel humiliated? He did bring me here, though. What right do I have to demand money from him? If he doesn't give me any, that means he doesn't feel the need to. Even though he says that he is glad I came, there is no question that I am a nuisance to him. Maybe I'd better go back early. Three weeks under these conditions will be a long nightmare. The prospect of returning to the kibbutz, talking to my friends, seeing my girlfriend, did warm my heart. But if I returned immediately, what would I answer them — what would I answer myself —

when asked: "Well, what did you think of your father after twenty years? Did you find anything in common? Did you feel any love for him?" I couldn't lie. We were still facing the challenge. It was too soon to return. We couldn't part as strangers. Maybe he wasn't interested in his only son. Or he couldn't break his habits overnight and behave like a loving father. The only people he seemed to really love were the heroes of his stories. He could talk about them for hours. If I wanted to know my father, I would have to enter his inner world. But how do you get to know a world that is so strange and distant? It was all a bit discouraging.

A few days later, looking through the thick Manhattan phone book, I found the New York address of Ha-Shomer Ha-Tsa'ir, the American chapter of the socialist Zionist movement I belonged to. Its office was on 88th Street, not far from my father's apartment on Central Park West and 101st Street. In recent years I had been a youth leader in the movement, and I hoped that I could find some work there, perhaps as a counselor, which would make my stay in New York not only more independent but also more pleasant.

The next day, feeling motivated, I hurried down to the three-story brownstone on 88th Street. Young people in the blue trademark shirts of the movement were running around and arguing vehemently about all sorts of things.

"You speak Hebrew?" I asked a man who was walking by me.

"Of course. I'm David Livni from Kibbutz Hatsor. I'm the central representative of the movement here."

We shook hands. I was a member of Kibbutz Beit-Alfa, I told him, and had had some experience in educational work.

"Beit-Alfa? How did you get into America?"

"With a passport that says I'm an artificial inseminator from Haifa."

"Artificial inseminator? So what are you doing here?" shouted one of the students.

Members of Ha-Shomer Ha-Tsa'ir were considered to be communists and weren't allowed into the United States, I explained. In order to be able to come here, I had declared, on the advice of friends, that I was an artificial inseminator working at Ha-On, an institute for artificial insemination near Kibbutz Sarid. The director of the institute had been a member of my kibbutz and was glad to give me a certificate stating that I worked at the institute; he even invited me to spend a day there so that I'd be familiar with their work. I changed my address from the kibbutz to Haifa, where my mother was living, thus obliterating my kibbutz past.

One fine day, I put on a suit from the kibbutz clothing store and a tie from the Purim costume collection, wrapped myself in a coat so no one would see me in that outrageous and heretical getup, and went to the American consulate in Haifa. A clerk from the immigration service carefully examined my passport and showed some interest in my profession. My English wasn't sophisticated enough for me to explain my work to him. I found myself obliged to resort to gestures when he asked me to show him how it was carried out.

The clerk laughed uproariously. "Tell me something, do you enjoy this?" he asked with a roguish wink.

What could I answer?

"Somebody has to fertilize a cow in heat," I replied.

"But why you and not the bull?" he insisted.

I explained to him that you could fertilize a whole herd of cows with one portion of sperm, especially prize breeds. My answers apparently satisfied him. He granted me permission to enter the United States.

I was relieved that the Zionist movement agreed to find me

work. And before I knew it, I was sitting in on top leadership
meetings with members of the movement and representatives
from Israel. Some of the local kids knew Hebrew because they
had attended the leadership seminar in Israel. I told David Livni
who my father was, but it didn't seem to make any special
impression on him. Nonetheless, David was familiar with his
books. But when I told him where I lived, he said: "Central
Park West, eh? I guess you don't need anything!"

"No, no."

That day was the first since my arrival in New York that I
didn't have lunch with my father. I went instead to a restaurant
with the Zionist representatives and the students, with all of one
dollar in my pocket. After examining the menu carefully, I
ordered only a bowl of soup. "I'm not hungry," I explained, "I
had a big breakfast." While my companions devoured steak,
french fries, and other tempting things, I made do with soup.
One of the women who worked in the office and would soon
be immigrating to Israel asked me to teach her Hebrew. I was
delighted at the prospect of earning a little more money.

"Can you be at the office at seven tomorrow morning?" she
asked. "We start work at eight."

"Of course," I replied eagerly.

That evening I told my father of the job I had found and he
shook his head. "A Hebrew teacher at seven in the morning?"

"I'm used to getting up early."

"Fine," he said, and went back to his writing.

The next morning, it was raining. I ran the whole way and
showed up at her place at seven. If I took the subway and my
new student didn't pay me my salary that day, I wouldn't have
enough money for soup. But to my relief, when the lesson was
over, she handed me a dollar.

"I hope that's all right," she said. "I've got a lot of expenses in preparation for my immigration."

With more than a dollar in my wallet, I felt rich and decided to celebrate with a trip to Times Square. Emerging from the subway, I discovered myriad electronics stores and spent a great deal of time dreaming that I might someday buy a radio. We had only one radio on the kibbutz; it was in the dining hall, and people always congregated around it.

Everything about Times Square dazzled me. I marveled at the cowboy who blew eternal smoke rings atop a gigantic pack of Camels. How did they do that? Illuminated news headlines were coming from one of the buildings, up high, under the roof. There were some Khrushchev declarations that I couldn't understand. I walked on. A priest at a street corner urgently called on Jesus to save mankind.

As I continued, a prostitute in a very short skirt grabbed my crotch and whispered in my ear: "Hey man, wanna fuck me?"

"No, no," I shouted in a panic, pushing her hand away. Maybe the priest was right after all.

In one of the electronics stores, I discovered television for the first time and stood in front of the set, mesmerized. There was Charlie Chaplin on the screen, tottering on his walking stick. I watched in awe for a long time — and must have looked the hick that I was.

My relations with my father continued to be frozen. I would leave my father's house early in the morning and come back at night. My daily lunches consisted of soup and rolls, and I seemed to be losing weight. Coming home one day, I found my father in an exceptionally good mood. The reason for his good spirits, Alma told me, was that he had sold a story for a thousand dollars.

"A thousand dollars," I repeated the sum in disbelief. It seemed so much to me. I congratulated him, and he smiled his thanks.

"Tell me, aside from Marxist literature, have you also read some of my books?"

"Yes. *Satan in Goray* and *The Family Moskat.* I didn't like *Satan in Goray. The Family Moskat* was OK."

"What didn't you like about *Satan in Goray?*" he asked.

"Your writing is mystical, full of sex, and doesn't reflect Jewish life in Poland."

"How do you know?" he asked curiously.

"I read your brother I. J. Singer's books. He talks about the Jewish proletariat, the class struggle in the textile mills of Lodz, and the war against capitalist exploitation."

My father laughed. "Abe Cahan, the editor of the Yiddish daily, *The Forward,* also wants me to write about the professional struggle of the Jews. Someday you'll wake up, my son, and see with your own eyes how your Marxism is sinking, and then maybe you'll understand that literature isn't 'socialist realism' or political posters, like in Russia," he commented sarcastically.

"That's how every imperialist and reactionary interprets the revolution, and I see that you're no different. The economic success of the Soviet Union is a thorn in your flesh," I answered.

Sensing a bitter argument about to begin, Alma begged my father not to be too hard on me.

At the end of my first week there, I had had enough and decided to go back to Israel. I had no reason to stay in New York. Along with everything else, I couldn't stand the fact that my father was also a reactionary. The barrier between us seemed to have become impenetrable. I racked my brain trying to find what we possibly had in common aside from blood. He was a capitalist and I was a socialist. He was a luftmensch living on air, and I was a fisherman who lived on the kibbutz by the sweat of my brow. He was a Yiddishist who wrote in a dead language, and I was an Israeli who spoke modern Hebrew. He was the embodiment of the Diaspora, and I rejected the Diaspora. He believed in demons, ghosts, and all kinds of superstitions; I was a materialist, a rationalist. I knew that back in Poland, he had starved himself almost to death to avoid serving in the Polish army, whereas I was a proud soldier who had fought in the Israeli War of Independence. Did I have to grope my way to him just because he had sired me? Our worlds were different, and it didn't look as if the gap that separated them could ever be bridged.

"Gigi, what do you do there on the kibbutz?" he asked.

"I'm a fisherman."

"A fisherman? Since when have Jews been fishermen?" He fell into deep thoughts. "Maybe when they lived on the rivers of Babylon? Fishing isn't a Jewish profession. The New Testament mentions fishermen from Lake Kinneret," he recalled. Suddenly, he switched to Hebrew. "Gigi, are there any women in your life?"

"No. There are no women in my life. Only one girl, and she works in the cow barn on the kibbutz."

"A cowherd?"

"She works in the cow barn."

Conversations with him exhausted me. At that time, I didn't understand that that was his way of trying to get closer to his son.

One day as I was eating my usual lunch with the movement

group, David Livni remarked that I was again eating only soup and bread. "Tell me, do you need money?" he asked. "Let me treat you to lunch."

"What do you mean? I don't need money." I felt myself blushing. My pride wouldn't let me admit my penurious condition.

"Can you drive a truck?" David asked.

"I worked as a driver on the kibbutz and took milk cans to the dairy cooperative in Tel Yosef three times a day. I've got an international license to drive a truck."

"Great! Can you start tomorrow?"

The next day, David suggested that I take some kitchen equipment to Liberty, New York, where the movement ran a summer camp.

"No problem. But somebody has to show me how to get to Liberty."

"Take a hundred dollars for gas, tolls, and other expenses."

"A hundred dollars? What'll I do with so much money?"

"Buy yourself some rolls and a whole pot of soup." He smiled.

That evening my father asked me if I needed money, and handed me a dollar bill.

"No thanks," I said.

"Take it, take it. In America you never refuse money." He tried to coax me and stuck the bill in my shirt pocket. I gave him back the money. He seemed offended. I stuck my hand in my pocket and pulled five twenty-dollar bills out of my wallet.

"Where did you get so much money?" my father shouted. "Did you rob a bank?"

"I'm a truck driver."

"A truck driver? Alma, come fast. Look at Gigi, my son. A truck driver. He just came to America and already he's a success. He did that! He's all right!" He became very excited. I could see that, for the first time, he was proud of his son. He got up from the sofa, came over to where I was standing, and hugged me warmly. Could the fact of my earning money be the reason for his excitement? I didn't understand. Was money the cause for his change? Had he been testing me?

4

DEMONS AND GHOSTS AT STEINBERG'S

The denizens of Broadway were used to seeing him walking in the afternoon with a bag of seeds in his pocket. Now and then he'd stop and survey the roofs of the tall, slanted buildings, searching for his friends the pigeons; when he saw them, he'd take a handful of seeds from his bag and scatter them on the curb. A flock of hungry pigeons would land at his feet and pounce eagerly on the food. He'd look at them mildly, enjoy their gluttony, and smile: "These pigeons are God's creatures. Which of us can be sure he won't come back as a winged creature in the next life?"

This phrase epitomized my father's credo, which combined the upper worlds and the lower worlds in an inseparable union. His feet walked in the twentieth century, but his ears were tuned to secret, mysterious voices.

"Do you really believe in those forces?" I asked as we were strolling in Manhattan a couple of weeks after I had arrived. He smiled as if to say, you won't believe your ears anyway.

"Yes, I do believe those forces exist. We don't see them, but they're an integral part of our lives. I don't know for sure who is a demon and who is a ghost. Those are just names, but ghosts and demons are an intrinsic part of our experience. Sometimes those forces are benevolent and help us, and sometimes they're malevolent and work against us. If you like, it's the perversion of reality. I think that in the future, it will be proved that these creatures aren't folklore but tangible facts."

We stood still. He pulled the bag of seeds out of his coat pocket and started scattering them over the sidewalk on 96th Street. Hungry pigeons swooped down on us, and one of them even landed on my father's hat. He laughed like a child; he believed that the pigeons knew him and were waiting impatiently for him every day. "A pigeon wouldn't land on the head of just anyone on Broadway. With their divine intuition, they can distinguish a Jewish writer, and they're sure he won't do anything to hurt them."

The cop on the beat appeared in the distance. My father quickly stuffed the bag into his coat pocket, and we took off. Apparently his fear of the authorities hadn't subsided over the years. If you've ever lived in a country illegally, you never get over your fear of the officials.

We entered Steinberg's restaurant and sat down at my father's usual table in the corner. The owner, an old acquaintance of his, greeted him warmly. My father pointed to me with a hint of pride: "That's my son, from Eretz-Israel. Came on a visit."

The restaurant owner gawked at us. "Mister Singer," he said, "you never told me you had a son in Israel."

"Oh yes, there're lots of things I haven't told you." He smiled.

We ordered coffee and apple pie. It was a cold, wintry day, and only after we both had warmed up a bit did I feel comfortable enough to start asking him questions. Ever since I had started working for the movement, our relations had improved. I yearned to get to know him, as a son knows a father. Did he really believe those superstitions? As a Marxist, I simply couldn't understand it. I glanced all around and then felt brave enough to ask: "Look, nobody's listening to us, and I swear I'll never tell your secret. Do you really and truly believe in demons and ghosts, or is that some literary 'trick' you use to deal with complicated subjects that have no rational solution?"

He smiled at me and dismissed the question with his familiar wave of the hand. He probably thought that an argument with me on those subjects was a total waste of time. "I know that materialists like you consider demons and ghosts as superstitions. But you should know that there are many scientists today who have come across facts that they can neither explain nor deny." Materialists, he said, dubbed them with names like telepathy, intuition, instinct, and so forth. "But these forces are with us all the time, and if you don't have them, you're not a person. Without them, there's no love. You've got a girlfriend in Israel, right?"

I nodded. In one of my letters, I had told him about her. My father believed that when a man and a woman love each other, there is such communication that they can almost read each other's mind. There is no love without telepathy, he kept telling me, just as there is no knowledge without instinct. "Haven't you sometimes known exactly what your girlfriend was thinking without her telling you?"

"Often," I replied.

He smiled.

My father cut a piece of apple pie and took a sip of coffee. We remained silent for a while. "There are a lot of things we can't explain," he continued. He told me of a woman from the town of Bilgoray. That woman had never heard about the lottery. One night she dreamed that her husband had won five hundred zlotys in a lottery near Lublin. She went to my mother and told her about her dream. A week later, her husband went to Lublin and found out that he had won five hundred zlotys. "Have you got an explanation for that?" he asked.

"No, I don't. Are you sure the story's true?"

"I knew the woman."

He shifted the conversation: "I believe that souls come out of their graves at midnight and unite with demons and ghosts. Gigi, would you be willing to stand guard all alone at midnight in the huge cemetery in Queens? Wouldn't you be scared?"

"No, I wouldn't be scared. It may not be my favorite place to be at midnight. I've spent many nights in ambushes in the Negev, the only guard awake across from an Egyptian fortification."

My father thought that men like Newton came to their insights not only because of their genius but also with the help of hidden forces some call instinct. "Can you explain to me what 'instinct' is?" he asked.

A bee flew into the restaurant and over to our table. It slowly circled my father's pie, buzzing loudly. At first, my father was scared; then he became interested in the trajectory of the bee's flight. He wanted to understand its motives, the reason it appeared in Steinberg's, of all places. Finally the bee landed on his plate and began advancing on the pie.

"We know the bee makes honey," he said, and pointed at it. He asked if I could explain to him how it does that. Sometimes it passes up hundreds of blooming flowers until it finds its way to one specific flower miles away from the hive. To say that its instincts lead it doesn't explain what instinct is. Suddenly the bee rose up and began circling. My father was jittery and waved his hands to drive it away. When the bee took off, he said: "Who knows what made it want to sting a Jewish writer?"

People came and went. We stayed a while at Steinberg's. It

was past lunch hour. Raising his eyes to the ceiling and speaking half to me, half to himself, my father said: "If the Angel of the Lord came down straight to Steinberg's right now, I imagine the scientists would give him a name and integrate him into their scientific world. When we substituted the word 'nature' for 'God,' we really didn't do anything," he explained. "Because what, in fact, is nature? How does it work? What are its laws? Are its forces seen? What keeps it going? The difference between us and religious people is that we call the unknown nature, and they call it God. All our knowledge of the world is practical. We know how to use some of the rules of nature, but it's only an external use."

"Did your brother think that way too?"

"No, no. By the way, his wife Genia called me yesterday. I told her you were here. She wants to see you very much. She remembers you from Warsaw, when you were five. Do you remember her?"

"No."

"If you like, we can visit her. No, maybe you'd better go alone. She lives nearby. I haven't got any time for visits."

We left the restaurant. A cold west wind blew from the Hudson, and brown leaves fallen off the trees of the boulevard whirled about. My father lifted his head and began looking for his pigeons. Some of them were clinging to the windows against the wind in the upper floors of the buildings, looking down with their pigeonlike tranquility.

"They're waiting for us," he said, and pulled out his seeds. Once again the pigeons came down to us from all sides. People with their coats buttoned and their collars up hurried by, glancing at us, amused: they have time to feed the pigeons? The wind grew stronger, and my father had to hang on to his hat with one hand and scatter seeds with the other. He spoke Yiddish to the pigeons, convinced that they understood him. One big bird stood at a distance, glaring at us, and didn't join the feast. My father tossed a handful of seeds at him, but that character didn't deign to come close, shaking his head in a firm refusal. Then he spread his wings and took off.

"That saint refuses to accept human gifts," declared my father.

We returned home, where he relaxed in his armchair, as usual. His blue eyes seemed to become less blue in the dim room. A few beams of light illuminated his face. Piles of books, newspapers, and magazines were stacked high everywhere in the living room — on the shelves, on the desk, on the floor. The many translations of his books lined the shelves. "Yiddish," I couldn't help remarking, "is a language that is either dead or dying, and one that received a mortal wound in the Holocaust. Without translation, only a few people would be able to read your books."

"You might not know it," said my father, "but Hebrew was also a dead language for two thousand years. But a miracle happened, and it came back to life. We can't know whether such a miracle won't happen to Yiddish. There are still a lot of Jews in the world who read Yiddish. I know that Yiddish is a language of the past, but even if I'm its last writer, I'll go on writing in Yiddish," he proclaimed emotionally.

I pulled *Satan in Goray* off the shelf and leafed through it. When the book had appeared in Hebrew, I had still been in high school on the kibbutz, and I remember the teacher who told me about it. I was so excited, I ran to the library. I would at last be able to read something my father had written! I opened it at random to a chapter titled "A Wedding on a Dung-Hill" and was immediately embarrassed. In those days, we were ardent believers in socialist realism. We eagerly read such books as

The Brave Red Star, Far from Moscow, and anything that glorified socialism in the Soviet Union. We believed that literature was integral to the construction of the regime. I read my father's book in secret, embarrassed by the descriptions of sex. I wasn't emotionally prepared to respond to the work. I was reserved and ashamed, and I buried the book under my mattress so the other boys wouldn't read it and tease me. Ten years later, in New York, I told my father about that.

"Hiding a book so it won't be read is like burning it," he said.

"Why are you so preoccupied with sex in your books," I couldn't resist asking, "and why are you so eager to put soft yeshiva students in bed with shiksas? Is that typical of the shtetl?"

Even in the Bible, he explained, there are stories about sex and lust. It wasn't he who had put a shiksa in the rabbi's bed; the authors of the Bible had already done that. They were the ones who put shiksas in bed with our kings and weren't ashamed of it, because you don't have to be ashamed of anything human, he insisted. They wrote about sex, about lust, about murder, in a language that was often obscure, he continued. There is no taboo against lust in the Jewish religion. Lust is frequently mentioned in the Bible. When the Prophets rebuked the people of Israel, they called them "whores" and "adulterers," but when they wanted to express love for their people, they used sexual symbols: God is the husband, and the nation is the "virgin of Israel." People who are disgusted by lust or sex aren't Jews!

We then talked about Jewish-Gentile relations, and my father expressed concern over the increasing number of mixed marriages in America.

"What's wrong with mixed marriages if people love each

other?" I asked. "Isn't real love stronger than religion or nationality?"

From his experience, most mixed marriages ended in divorce.

"The Jews aren't a race," he stated. "All of us were the grandsons not only of Jews but also of the other nations of the world. For two thousand years, we haven't been able to preserve racial purity. Foreign blood is mixed in us, and we don't ask a blue-eyed Jew if he's of pure race or not. The main thing is what that man feels in his heart and what people he wants to belong to. If a Gentile woman wants to be a Jew, the Talmud says she's one of us. As Ruth the Moabite said: 'Thy people shall be my people and thy God my God.' "

For him, such a Gentile woman was a Jew in every respect, whether she converted to Judaism or not. The main thing was her faith, even if it wasn't assumed for its own sake. But marriage for love, which was mainly sensual, usually didn't turn out well, he maintained. "If the stranger comes to us in his own spirit, in his own identity, he is one of us. But if the Jew goes away from us, he turns into a stranger. The sons of Esau and Ishmael were also the sons of our father Abraham, but they don't belong to us, since they took another path. It's harder to make a match for a man than to part the Red Sea, and with the daughter of another people, it's seven times harder."

It wasn't that my father considered love between a Jewish man and a Gentile woman a negative thing. If the Gentile woman, he explained to me, joined us, that love was considered positive, since many of us are the offspring of mixed unions anyway. "Don't forget that King David is descended from Ruth the Moabite, who was a symbol of sainthood."

The last sunbeams glowed. We sat in silence for a while.

Over the years, he elaborated these ideas in such books as *The Slave,* with Wanda and Jacob; *The Magician of Lublin,* with Magda and Yasha; and *Enemies, a Love Story,* with Yadwiga and Herman.

5

LABOR PAINS OF A STORY

Writing, and writing stories in particular, remained something of a mystery to me. I often wondered how a story was born. And even as the son of a writer, the process of creating a literary work was a big puzzle to me. How do ideas take shape? I asked him again and again. My father didn't have any answers to such questions, as if it was a mystery for him as well. Each of his creations had emerged in different ways. There was no pattern.

During the first visit, when I stayed with him in New York, I tried to pierce that mystery by keeping an eagle eye on my father and observing his daily routine. My father would wake up at seven o'clock every morning and lie in bed for another two hours, thinking — I found out — about the story he was working on at the time. On the nightstand next to his bed were notebooks he constantly filled with ideas, expressions, synonyms, anything he felt he needed for his stories. I would often see him close his eyes as he was straining to come up with the right word or a peculiar twist of phrase; when a smile spread over his face, I knew that he had found the solution to whatever problem he had been pondering. By the time those two hours of concentration were over, the story was thoroughly structured and woven, with all its details.

At nine o'clock, he put his thin feet on the scale next to his bed and examined the needle for a long time to make sure he hadn't put on any weight. When he was reassured that all was in good order, he hurried to the bathroom and soaked in hot water for half an hour, still deep in thought and, I guessed, completing the creative process. After his bath, wrapped in a gray robe, he would hurry to the kitchen for a hasty breakfast. Obsessed with his story and eager to get it down on paper, he pulled out his chair, sat down, and wrote page after page without stopping. I could see his face reflecting the emotions of his heroes: he would rejoice with them, enjoy their witty repartee, and a moment later I would catch him tormented when catastrophe struck them. Every few minutes, it seemed, the phone would ring. Usually it was one of his fans from Brooklyn or the Bronx who wanted to discuss his last story in *The Forward*. Soon into the conversation they'd relate their own troubles, and my father would shake his head and mutter in Yiddish. After hanging up, he would run back to his chair and continue his writing as if nothing had interrupted him.

These telephone conversations never seemed to bother him. He didn't mind dropping everything to pick up the phone, as if he expected to hear some marvelous news. When he was in the process of writing a story that had already been completed in his mind, it wasn't hard for him to leave it momentarily. He was always able to pick up where he had left off. By afternoon, he usually stopped writing. What surprised me most was that he never reread what he had written; he just checked whether the pages were numbered properly. He'd put the manuscript in a stamped envelope and send it off to his American translator.

"How is it that you don't go over what you write?" I asked him. "Is your writing so perfect that there aren't any mistakes or repetitions? No sentences to cut out?"

"The material will come back to me in the English translation, and then I'll polish every sentence."

The next day, someone from *The New Yorker* called. One of
the editors who was fluent in Yiddish had translated the story
for the editor in chief, who had accepted it for publication.

With a smile on his face one day, and as if to answer my
recurring questions about how his stories were born, he told
me that when he was working on *Scum,* he had managed to
bring himself back to Poland, where he relived the Jewish
underworld of Warsaw he had seen as a young man. He identified so deeply with his characters that at times he heard himself
talking like the thieves and butchers he was writing about.
Slang expressions of the Warsaw pimps kept flashing back in his
memory, and he found himself cursing out loud like them.
"There were times I even heard prostitutes cajoling passersby
on Krochmalna Street."

A story wasn't born all at once, he told me. First he needed a
plot, and for him, it was easier if it was a love story. Once he
settled on a love story, he always preferred a tale of adultery.
Married love, he said, simply isn't as strong as the clandestine
version. But the writing didn't always flow for him. There were
often times when one of his ideas simply couldn't be turned
into a story, and the plot inevitably got stuck. Several hundred-
page novels whose plots had come to a dead end were tucked
away. When he talked about it, he compared one of his unfinished stories to a broken motor that was better to junk than to
repair.

"If I'm embarking on a story, I've got to be convinced, or at
least believe, that I'm the only one who can write it. I need to
feel a strong urge to write it. It also has to express my world, and
my faith as a writer. If one of these elements is missing, I won't
write the story."

Every character he described in his works emanated from real experience. I know, for I have witnessed it with my own eyes or heard him tell me about events in his life. He had to have known someone to be able to describe that person and lead him on the paths of his imagination. All my father seemed to need was a grain of truth to construct a fictitious plot. I remember, for example, one day when we were in a cafeteria on Broadway. Sitting at one of the tables in the corner was a woman in her sixties with a long white beard, smoking a cigar. Neither my father nor I could take our eyes off her. "I sense that she's got a fascinating story," he whispered to me. A friend of my father's entered the restaurant, and my father asked him to introduce him to her. He moved to her table and ended up talking with her for hours. For the rest of that day, he remained preoccupied with the bearded woman. Not long after that encounter, his story "The Beard" came out.

> Then someone knocked at my door. I opened it and what I saw was like a nightmare. Outside stood a woman dressed in a shabby black dress, men's shoes, and a hat, with a white beard. She leaned on a cane. I knew at once who she was — Mrs. Pupko. . . . She took out a cigar and lit it. Perhaps it's a man, I thought. But I saw that she had a large bust. Probably androgynous, I thought.

The plot, of course, had its own Singer twists and turns, but the sight of the woman and the few biographical details my father had been able to obtain from her were enough for him to weave his rich, fictional tale. The Mrs. Pupko of "The Beard" really did exist. I saw her with my own eyes.

My father was in the habit of writing his books one or two

chapters at a time, and as these chapters were finished, they were published in *The Forward*. Every week he was expected to hand in a two-thousand-word story to the newspaper. After the book was completed and he had read its English translation, only then was he able to see its shortcomings: a plot that had worked so well for him in Yiddish didn't automatically hold together in English. He'd go back to his desk, rewrite it, and adjust it for the English reader. Sometimes, when his heroes were caught up in their troubles and he had a hard time finding a way out for them, he would stop work on the novel for a week. He would often write an entirely new story, go back to the novel, and insert the story. Every now and then he would even ask me how I would finish a particular story. These were precious moments, when the two of us would sit and elaborate on his writing.

In *Yentl, a Yeshiva Boy,* my father couldn't decide how to end the hopeless love between Yentl and Avigdor. I suggested a happy ending: the two of them would run away from the city and their respective spouses; at dusk, sweating and tired, they would come to a river, take off their clothes, and the naked truth would be revealed to them. My father smiled and commented: "Only a rationalist like you believes in a happy ending. In real life, things don't happen as we'd like. They suffer a bitter fate, and all they can do is disappear, leaving behind an unforgettable tangle."

Was there a connection between my father's experiences and his stories? I often asked him that question, but he'd always shrug his shoulders and wouldn't answer. I accompanied him one time to the offices of *The Forward* as he was delivering one of his chapters. He usually sent his material by mail, but because of some holiday that week, he had no time to wait for postal delivery. The typesetter had warned him that if he didn't have my father's story within the hour, he wouldn't have time to set it. My father picked up an envelope from his desk, and we set out. Arriving at *The Forward*, he pulled out his manuscript with a smile; then, all of a sudden, I saw him turn pale. The envelope contained the wrong manuscript. He called home immediately, only to learn that the cleaning woman had thrown the good manuscript into the garbage. There was no copy. He was terribly upset. That week, of course, the two chapters didn't appear, and my father received angry phone calls from his readers.

Years later, I came across his story "Manuscript," about a bohemian writer named Menashe Linder and his mistress Shivta, an actress. The story takes place at the outbreak of the war, when the couple is fleeing Warsaw with a suitcase containing the manuscript of Menashe's new book, which Shivta describes as a literary pearl. The story recounts the hardships of their journey to Bialystok, which was occupied by the Soviets. There, Menashe was going to have an opportunity to publish his book and receive a considerable advance. But when the suitcase is opened, it turns out that, instead of Menashe's book, it contains the manuscript of some novice writer, and the devoted Shivta walks all the way back to Warsaw to retrieve the manuscript. She reaches Warsaw, eventually finds the right manuscript, and hurries back to Bialystok with it. She reaches the city early in the morning and finds Menashe in bed with another woman. She pulls the manuscript out from under her shirt, opens the door of the oven, and tosses it in.

"What about the time when I was visiting you in New York, and you brought the wrong manuscript to *The Forward*? Is there any connection between these events?" I asked my father.

He smiled. "Maybe."

"A writer," my father often said to me, "like a yeshiva boy,

has to set times for Torah." He set strict times for his writing and
didn't rely on inspiration. "A writer's like a horse; he has to be
whipped all the time. He also needs a tight schedule that will
force him to submit his material on time."

One autumn day, we were sitting on a bench on Broadway
under a tree. A strong wind was blowing, and the leaves were
falling. My father directed my attention to two remaining leaves
struggling against the wind, which was doing its best to pluck
them off the branch. The leaves kept coming together and
separating. There had to be a stormy affair between the big leaf
and the small leaf, he concluded. The wind continued to blow
harder, and the leaves touched and caressed lightly, like a loving
couple. My father couldn't take his eyes off them. His ears heard
their secret love conversation. This little episode later became a
story that I translated into Hebrew.

Father, how is a story born? I asked again and again. And
glancing at me with his soft blue eyes, he always replied:
"Sometimes with labor pains, sometimes even by cesarean, but
mostly for me, peacefully and calmly, like a ship cruising on a
placid sea.

"Personally," he told me once, "it's not the writing that's the
problem, but the ability to weave an interesting, authentic plot.
Ideas pop up all the time. The human brain works twenty-four
hours a day, whether we're awake or dreaming. Most of the
ideas are forgotten. But if we can succeed in taming the human
mind to leave us something, we can benefit from it. Let's go to
Steinberg's," he suggested. "I invited a refugee to lunch."

And that refugee turned into Masha of *Enemies, a Love Story.*

6

AUNT GENIA

One day, as I was walking in New York during one of my visits, an elderly woman stopped me on the street and asked me: "Excuse me, are you Gigi?"

In New York, with its eight million inhabitants, you would not think it likely that you would run into a person who remembers your nickname from twenty years ago in Warsaw. "I'm Genia, your aunt, the wife of I. J. Singer. Your father told me you were here. I invited the two of you to come over, but your father, as always, promises and doesn't keep his word. Oh, you look so much like him, but you also look like Ronia, your mother. Come with me, we'll buy some apple pie and go to my house. I live right here, around the corner." I followed behind her, startled by the chance encounter in the gigantic city.

I had not known my uncle. He had left Poland in 1933 when I was four years old. Genia and her husband apparently used to come to our house at 57 Leszno Street often and play with me. She kept repeating that I was a "wonderful child." Since then, we hadn't seen each other, and it was all the more astonishing that after all these years she had been able to identify me. She even remembered our address in Warsaw. She was still angry at my father for leaving my mother and me in Warsaw. She and her husband Joshua had often tried to persuade him to devote more time to us, to no avail.

I knew my uncle I. J. Singer only through his books, which had thrilled me when I read them in my youth. I had been infinitely more proud of him than of my father, I remember. I often read his *Yoshe Kalb, The Brothers Ashkenazi,* and *The Family Carnovsky.* When I taught high school on the kibbutz, I would read chapters of *Yoshe Kalb* to my students. The book gave them a new perspective on Hasidic life and the shtetl in Eastern Europe.

And here I was, sitting in my aunt Genia's house, drinking coffee, eating apple pie, and glancing at the pictures on the wall. There was something so strange, I thought, about traveling halfway around the world to meet a father I had never known, and then also discovering another branch of my family tree here with Genia Singer. I asked her to tell me about her late husband. Joshua, she said, had dreamed of becoming a painter. Their son, Yossele, was the one with an extraordinary talent. "You want to see some of his pictures?" she asked.

"Later. There's time," I replied, and urged her to continue.

"I'm so glad you came. As for our story, I don't know where to begin. Do you know that our oldest son Yasha died in Poland of pneumonia when he was fourteen?"

"No."

"Your father didn't write to you about it?"

"Maybe he did, but I don't remember."

Yasha's death had been very hard for them. Even my father, Genia said, had loved him very much. He would never get over the premature deaths of her husband and her son, he had told her.

Her husband realized early on that he wouldn't be able to make a living as a painter and switched to literature. At the age of twenty-five, he worked for the journal *The Jewish Word* and was an ardent believer in Soviet communism.

"You're from a kibbutz, right?"

"Right." As a young socialist, I told her, I had identified closely with her husband's feelings for social justice in his book *The Brothers Ashkenazi,* which vividly describes the struggles of the Jewish revolutionary Nissan.

Genia stood up and kissed me. "Nissan was my husband," she said excitedly. He had poured all the enthusiasm of his revolutionary faith into that character. Had I turned away from Stalin and cut myself off from "phony communism," she wanted to know.

I wasn't sure that it was "phony communism," I answered, adding that the government of the Soviet Union suffered from isolation and had many difficulties. I believed, however, that the regime was concerned primarily with the workers and would find a way to relieve the Russian proletariat.

She chuckled. "Your naïveté reminds me so much of my husband's. He could never accept the facts of life. There was a lot of corruption and bureaucracy there." My uncle Joshua had had continual arguments in the Writers' Club in Warsaw. He fervently justified the regime, until he and Genia immigrated to the Soviet Union, where they spent two years. "Your mother Ronia was also a communist once. You were really lucky to get thrown out of there."

In 1919, shortly after the Revolution, they went to the Soviet Union, where Joshua found work on a newspaper, *The New Times,* and was considered one of the "Kiev writers." Then they moved to Moscow, where he published articles and stories. But when it came time to pay him his royalties, his editors asked him to give up part of his wages "for the emerging socialism." Those were two very hard years, and in 1921 they returned to

Warsaw. By then, Joshua was thoroughly skeptical about the kind of regime they were building in the Soviet Union. Six years later, Abe Cahan, the editor of *The Forward,* suggested that he go back to the Soviet Union and report on developments in that country. The rumors of mass exiles to Siberia, and of massacres of thousands of peasants who were refusing to give up their land, were troubling the intelligentsia in Poland.

When Singer returned to Poland, he wrote a series of highly critical articles about Stalin's reign of terror. In 1969, his novel *Steel and Iron,* describing that period, was first published in English.

What were the relations between the two brothers? I asked Genia. But she didn't feel that she could confide in me and remained vague. She considered my father an ungrateful man. Joshua had felt responsible for my father's fate. Having been the first to abandon the Orthodox Jewish tradition, he thought that he had drawn my father along. They had very different temperaments, Genia told me. Joshua was known as a courageous, decisive rationalist who had made a final break with God; his brother, on the other hand, was a mystic who entertained himself with the notion that the world wasn't created according to the theory of evolution but directed by a divine hand. I detected a trace of mockery in Genia's words. The brothers frequently argued in her house, and apparently, as she put it, "demons and ghosts never impressed my husband."

In his book *In My Father's Court,* my father describes bitter arguments between his brother Joshua and his parents when the boy declared that God didn't exist.

My father arrived in Warsaw in 1923, at the age of nineteen. He had been invited by his older brother, who had arranged to have him hired as a proofreader at the newspaper he edited, *Literary Pages.* Soon after my father's arrival in Warsaw, Joshua suggested that he dispense with the external trappings of the traditional Jewish appearance. My father shaved off his earlocks and discarded his *kapote,* the long black overcoat that is part of customary Jewish attire. Joshua introduced him to his cronies at the Warsaw Writers' Club. My father was shy and lacked self-confidence, Genia told me. "He was a soft, provincial yeshiva boy." She was convinced that my father was jealous of her husband's talent, his important position, and his success. Her husband was a strong man with steely eyes, radiating force; he was a confirmed optimist, a worldly man. My father, on the other hand, was a nihilist, a pessimist, and was frightened of life; he would talk mainly of death, the suicide of the human race, and the end of the world. It was clear that, to Genia, her husband was the talented brother. The Singer home in Warsaw, and later in Seagate in Brooklyn, became the center for writers, for theater people, for Jewish artists and general bohemia. Joshua invited his brother to those parties, but my father inevitably remained a shy and withdrawn wallflower. Joshua was the Polish correspondent for *The Forward* and made a respectable salary. My father was unemployed but wouldn't take any money from his brother. "Your father was ashamed that he couldn't support himself."

Joshua would show him passages of *Yoshe Kalb* as he was writing it and ask my father's opinion about them. My father hid all his writings from his brother. According to Genia, while her husband was alive, my father played second fiddle to his brother. Joshua was famous, and my father was generally referred to as "the younger brother of the great writer." That is why he added his mother's name, Bath Sheba, to his name and became "Bashevis."

"If Joshua hadn't died so young, at fifty, he would have gone much further than your father."

It became clear to me that Genia and my father weren't on

the best of terms. Back in Poland, my father had taken great pains to hide his private life from his family, never introducing his girlfriends to them. He hid the objects of his romance or lust in his rented apartment in Warsaw and continued the practice once he got to New York.

"Being married to your mother didn't stop him from living a merry other life. All Warsaw knew what he was up to, except his brother, who refused to believe it." Genia stressed again, in case I had forgotten, that if it hadn't been for her husband, who had brought him to America, my father would have shared the same fate as their brother Moshe and the rest of the family, who were all killed in the Holocaust. "He owes his life to us," she concluded.

In 1933, Abe Cahan invited Joshua to the United States to write for *The Forward*. Two years later, Joshua brought his brother Isaac. When he first arrived in this country, Genia recalled, my father was miserable. Back in Warsaw, he had left friends and lovers, and he also missed the Writers' Club. In New York, he was scared to leave the house for fear of not being able to find his way back, and worst of all, he didn't know a word of English. "A person whose life is words finds himself overnight without words, therefore robbed of his life." Day after day he would lie in bed, staring at the ceiling. When my father was offered manual labor, his brother advised him to refuse it because "he was destined for greatness," he told his wife. Moreover, he added, "he's got two left hands." At *The Forward*, had it not been for Joshua, Abe Cahan would have fired my father. When assigned to write about Jewish suffering on the Lower East Side, or about the terrible exploitation of the Jewish immigrants in the sweatshops, my father was unable to report accurately. In addition to his mysticism, he was incapable of respecting the typesetting schedule.

In 1938, my father wrote to my mother:

> It really doesn't surprise me that I have managed to
> learn English and have gotten close to English Amer-
> ica. English-speaking America also makes serious
> mistakes and has its own diseases. Yiddish America is
> hell: it oppresses you, but I'm trying to get away from
> it, as you can imagine. . . . I'm now working again
> and feel like a man who has avoided a great spiritual
> danger. Once and for all, I've put an end to the idea
> of the possibility of "making a living" out of belles
> lettres, and of publishing things in *The Forward*. I
> work a little bit at *The Forward,* do some technical
> work, translate a piece or two, but I wouldn't dream
> of publishing a novel in *The Forward* — God keep me
> from being a literary writer for *The Forward*. The very
> idea that a work of mine would be published in *The
> Forward* makes me want to shun literature. I hate their
> broken and vulgar Yiddish and their notions of litera-
> ture, their expertise, and their opinions in general.
> But I hope there will be some niche for the reader
> I'm writing for. I even believe that I'll become a
> success, in some sense.
>   . . . Meanwhile I'm still poor as a church mouse.
> But I sense that I've already gone through the worst.
> Aside from that, the problem of money — as you
> yourself say in your letter — isn't so important to the
> two of us. And from that point of view, I don't think
> we disagree.
>   . . . After I sent you 15 dollars, I didn't have a cent
> in my pocket to buy the basic necessities.

My father often talked to me about his brother, whom he admired. Agreeing with Genia, he was sure that Joshua would have written several marvelous books had he lived longer. "When I got the Nobel Prize, I felt my brother standing there with me on the stage in Stockholm, sharing the prize and celebrating the victory of Yiddish," he told me.

I told my father that I had read somewhere that the death of his older, famous brother had liberated him, in a way, from the dependency that had oppressed him. He dismissed that remark as utter nonsense. "I regarded Joshua as my teacher, my spiritual father, who guided me in my first steps. I admired his talent very much, and I was grateful to him for bringing me to America and for his help when I was starting out. But when I decided to stand on my own two feet, I got up and went my own way. At any rate, there was no sibling rivalry. We got along fine. I loved him very much." After a pause, he added: "Of course, when two brothers are in the same profession and work in the same place, there's bound to be tension and maybe even jealousy. We both wrote about Jews."

In the same letter he had written my mother, that picture seemed to be a bit different:

> My work at *The Forward* is always hanging by a thread. My brother won't lift a finger to help me. He says there is nothing he can do to help. I am condemned to be poor as a church mouse. In this sense, there is absolutely no difference between brothers and strangers. I'm sure that if my brother were also as poor as a church mouse, he would try to help me more. What can I do? That's how he is.

Further on, he adds:

> Here, of all places, my brother has achieved great
> success. Artistically, he is deteriorating (in my opin-
> ion), but he has succeeded in turning the deteriora-
> tion into an asset (*tugent*). I believe my silence is
> better.

The letter doesn't specify what my father meant by Joshua's
"deterioration," but he may have been alluding to his brother's
adaptation to the taste of his readers and editors. These two
passages, in any case, indicate that relations between the
brothers weren't uncomplicated in those days. But my father's
opinion of *The Forward* did change, and he became the "literary
artist" of the newspaper for the rest of his life.

My father considered his brother a typical rebel, a total
nonconformist who harshly criticized those parasitic Jews who
studied Torah day and night. Joshua thoroughly rejected the
traditional Orthodox notion that a Jew is born to study Torah,
arguing that those Jews had simply refused to leave the darkness
of the Middle Ages. "How long will you wait for the Messiah?"
Joshua had shouted, insisting that rabbis needed to prove that
the Torah had been given to Moses at Sinai. My uncle had fallen
in love with America the moment he had set foot on U.S. soil.
In an argument about the American proletariat, he proudly
declared that "in America, even in a pauper's house, you'll find
a bathtub."

"By the way, how did you find out about my brother Joshua's
death? Where were you then?" my father asked me, out of the
blue.

I had been in Israel, in a boarding school for adolescents — I
was fourteen years old — in the village of Shefiya, near

Zikhron Yaakov. Every year we had to clean the cesspools of the village, and naturally the stench was horrible. As a reward we got cigarettes. Our thought was that the smoke would mitigate the stink at least a little. So there I was one day, up to my knees in that muck, when the village manager appeared and held a long, whispered conversation with the supervisor. Every now and then they'd look over at me. Afraid that I was doing something wrong, I started being extra careful. Suddenly the supervisor's voice boomed out: "Singer, get out of the pit. Go take a shower and report to the manager's office!"

Reporting to the manager's office meant getting thrown out of the village. And I didn't know why. The children sadly said good-bye to me. I'd have to go back to Jerusalem and live in a rented room with my mother, who earned her living washing floors. After cleaning myself up, I anxiously knocked at the office door. The manager opened it, held out his hand, and invited me to sit down. He looked grave, and I trembled with fear. I tried to figure out what I had done wrong. I remembered stealing grapes from the vineyards of Zikhron Yaakov and plums from the orchards of the Arab village Faradis. Do they throw you out of the village for that? On the wall hung a picture of Henrietta Szold, the founding mother of the boarding school, and she seemed to be looking at me gently. That gave me heart. After a long silence, the manager pulled a copy of the newspaper *Davar* out of a drawer. He showed me a picture, with the caption: "I. J. Singer Dies of a Heart Attack."

"Israel Singer, I'm sorry to inform you that your father the writer has passed away," said the manager with a sad face. "On behalf of the village, I wish to express our condolences."

I breathed a sigh of relief that I wasn't being thrown out of the village. I bowed my head but didn't feel any grief.

"Your father passed away and you don't feel any grief?" my father commented years later, when I told him the story.

"At that time, I barely remembered that I had a father," I retorted.

On the table was a little basket of bananas and apples. The teachers used to buy fruit for themselves in Zikhron Yaakov. I kept staring at it, and as the silence continued, the manager offered me some fruit. The little basket was quickly emptied. I sat there, silent and embarrassed, not knowing what to say. Finally the manager asked if there was anything he could do to ease my grief. I realized that this was my opportunity to get out of cleaning the cesspools.

"I would like to mourn for my father by myself and not have to clean the village cesspools," I said, with a somber look on my face.

"Of course, that's obvious," answered the manager.

Upon learning that it was "obvious," I summoned up my courage for another request. "I'd also like to get the cigarettes the other children are getting."

"Yes, of course," the manager nodded, relieved that I had given him a chance to help an orphan lad. So, for three days, I read books, smoked cigarettes, and played the mandolin. The other children openly envied me.

"Your father dies and you celebrate," my father commented, shaking his head with a sad smile.

It took the manager two weeks to discover his error, and then he rushed to inform me that my father was still alive.

"Good material for a story," my father declared, with an amused look in his eyes.

When his brother died, my father felt bereft, he told me. His brother had been everything to him: father, brother, friend, and teacher. On the night before his death, February 9, 1944, they

met in a restaurant and had enjoyed themselves as usual. The
next day, Alma told him the bitter news. Later he wrote:

> I felt as if God had slapped my face. But what could I
> do, slap Him back? To this day, I don't understand
> why him and not me. Why didn't I devote more time
> to him? Why didn't we see each other more often?
> I am haunted by a feeling of guilt. Sometimes we
> seem to miss the important things of life. It's a feeling
> I can't get away from.

Some of his appreciation of his brother was expressed in the
dedication to his book *The Family Moskat:*

> I dedicate these pages to the memory of my late
> brother I. J. Singer, author of *The Brothers Ashkenazi.*
> To me he was not only the older brother, but a
> spiritual father and master as well. I looked up to him
> always as to a model of high morality and literary
> honesty. Although a modern man, he had all the
> great qualities of our pious ancestors.

7

SINGER, GET OUT

After my uncle I. J. Singer immigrated to America in 1933, he begged my father to join him. Hitler had taken power in Germany, and many Jews were fleeing for their lives. Russia wasn't the Garden of Eden either. Stalin was continuing his purges and exiles, and the Jews were his first victims. Poland clearly wouldn't be able to hold out for long as an independent state, and the winds of war were beginning to blow throughout Europe. The two brothers wrote a great deal to each other during that period. My father felt the ground burning under his feet and tried to get whatever papers he needed to leave Poland and go to America. My mother spoke of Palestine, but she really longed for the Soviet Union.

When I was five years old, I announced to the ice cream vendor across the street from our house in Warsaw that I was going to Palestine.

"Palestine?" said the man. "Only Zhids go there."

That night I asked my mother if I was a "Zhid," and she explained to me that there were good people who were workers and bad people who were exploiting capitalists. "Mother," I asked, "is the ice cream vendor a capitalist?"

"Of course. But don't worry, child. When the revolution comes, we'll take care of him."

In those years I heard a lot about that "revolution" from Mother, even though I didn't understand what she intended to revolutionize. All I really understood was that the worker was good and the capitalist was bad, and I have retained the revolutionary terminology ever since. Once, as a young child, I got mad at Father and called him a "capitalist." He picked me up, glared at me angrily, and asked: "Gigi, where did you get that word?"

"From Mother," I replied.

And they quarreled. They often quarreled, I remember. "Ronia, you're poisoning the child's soul," my father yelled at her.

Mother was a communist. The daughter of a rabbi, she had come a long way, like many Jewish girls who were educated in a Polish high school. Her fellow party members would visit our house in Warsaw, bringing manifestos and pamphlets embellished with a hammer and sickle. I remember that I used to draw them. Mother was careful to hide the material from my father, who always flew into a rage whenever he found communist propaganda in the house.

"They'll arrest me and I won't be able to go to America," he shouted at her. That was the first time I learned that he was planning to leave.

"Mother, are we going to America too?"

"Yes, child. Father will go first, and we'll come later."

But one day in 1932, someone denounced Mother. She was arrested for underground activities and spent two months in jail. The documents reveal that my father was also arrested and jailed for a day, but he was released when he proved his innocence. The event shook him profoundly. Mother's friends would take me to the street in front of the prison, where I called her name until she appeared at the barred window. I was even allowed to visit her in her cell. They barely let her kiss me. Two of her fellow party members, Klonya and Irka, were with me. My father had refused to come. He wouldn't forgive her for her political activity. Also, with her in jail, he had to assume the burden of taking care of me, which severely curtailed his activities. He didn't tell his cronies at the Writers' Club that she was in prison and forbade me to mention it. Mother's friends would sometimes come to our house and take care of me. Apparently, her imprisonment was the last straw for their marriage. After being released, Mother solemnly promised my father that she had put an end to that chapter of her life, but he didn't believe her. Soon after she was released, her friends began frequenting our home again the moment Father was out of the house.

One day when I was five years old, my father hugged and kissed me more warmly than usual; the bristles of his beard pricked my cheeks, and I asked him why he didn't shave. It was April 1935. I didn't see him again for twenty years.

A few months after he left, Mother and I took a long train trip to Moscow to stay with her younger sister, Manya. Once the train crossed the Russian border, on the embankment on both sides of the tracks, five-pointed stars and hammers and sickles carved in the rock accompanied us all the way. I knew these symbols from Mother's pamphlets. Security agents went through the compartments, examined documents, and asked questions. "Where's your father, little boy?" one of them asked me in broken Polish as he checked our documents. I was about to tell him that my father had sailed for America to be with his brother, the writer I. J. Singer, and that Mother and I were going to stay with Aunt Manya, when I felt a pinch on my leg that stopped my tongue. Mother explained to the man that my communist father was serving as party secretary of the Warsaw branch; he was detained there and would join us when he had finished his duties. That day, I learned that lying was a requirement for survival. When the security man left, I asked Mother why she had lied, and she attempted to explain that we mustn't tell anyone that Father had gone to "the capitalist country." He had gone to a bad place, and I understood that it was better not to talk about it.

Moscow, 1936, Red Square: I looked, and all around us I saw churches with gleaming onion-shaped domes. Along the wall there was a long line to the mausoleum. Snow. People were huddling on both sides of the road. A funeral was about to pass, we were told. Policemen stood in a row and kept order, their faces stern and tense. Mother explained to me that the distinguished writer Maxim Gorky had passed away. Suddenly the square fell silent and all hats came off, despite the bitter cold. My ears were freezing, and I begged Mother to let me put my hat back on. Glancing at the people around us, she said in a loud voice: "Honor the great writer, the blessed communist."

A cart drawn by six pairs of black horses slowly made its way, bearing a coffin draped in black. It was followed by only one man. From the picture in my kindergarten, I easily identified Joseph Stalin, striding slowly, with a gloomy expression on his face. I looked at the man with the mustache, the green military tunic, holding a visored cap, and I shouted: "Mother, look how little the great Stalin is!"

"Fool, snotty child!" people growled at me from all sides. One of them was pinching my behind hard. I burst into tears. The policemen in front of us apparently didn't hear or chose not to hear the comments of a little boy. Mother quickly shut me up and carefully assessed the people around us. She'd better get away fast, one man whispered to Mother, because "who knows what else that child is liable to do." When Stalin passed in front of us, everyone bowed deeply, and Mother made sure that I too bent down. Some women crossed themselves, and an orchestra played the funeral march. Stalin was followed at a distance by Gorky's thin widow, dressed in black mourning. After the funeral, we hurried out of the square. The following days, we lived in fear, jumping at every knock on the door. Mother had packed two suitcases in case we were expelled.

In the summer of 1937, about a year and a half after we had arrived in Russia, a secret police agent came to our house with an expulsion order. Mother couldn't understand what crime she had committed against the regime she had supported so fervently. Was it because of what her son had blurted out at Gorky's funeral? Or maybe it was because, at an editorial meeting of the Moscow Yiddish newspaper, *Soviet Homeland,* she had argued that the Jewish minority had historical rights, and that some of those rights were realized in Birobijan and some in Eretz-Israel. Perhaps someone had denounced her for her "reactionary" views. Since we were citizens of Poland, the authorities decided not to exile us to Siberia, but we were ordered to leave the Soviet Union within twenty-four hours.

Mother sent a cable to her own mother in Palestine, and the answer quickly came: "Go to Istanbul, entry visa to Palestine is on the way." That banishment shook Mother's faith in the party and her loyalty to its precepts; she never forgave them till the day she died. In retrospect, we were lucky because the Moscow trials and the purges against the "enemies of the people" were at their height, and the Soviet Union subsequently locked its gates and didn't let anyone out. The next day we took the train to Odessa, and from there we sailed to Istanbul.

We reached Istanbul with practically no money. We were

allowed to stay in Turkey for only forty-eight hours, and we took a room in a cheap hotel near the port, assuming that we would sail for Palestine in a day or two. Our room was in the attic, on the fourth floor, and we soon discovered that the lower three floors served as a whorehouse, where shouts and loud music blared all night long. Policemen were in and out, dealing with the drunken brawls. The forty-eight hours turned into an eternity. We stayed in Turkey illegally for nine months, fearing every sound, every knock on the door. I was forbidden to speak Russian so as not to reveal that we were refugees from Russia. Mother talked Polish with me again, and if I replied in Russian, she got angry. Every morning, I had to go to the YTA travel agency and ask if the visa had arrived. My mother taught me to ask in French, because the people there didn't know either Polish or Russian. It was the only French sentence I ever learned, and I remembered it for years.

In his first letter to Eretz-Israel, my father wrote:

Dear Ronia,

I'm very glad you are now in Palestine, despite recent events there that worry me. There is no peace in the world. What can you do? Let's hope that everything will work out for the best. I sent you a letter in Istanbul with a check for 20 dollars, but I'm sure you won't get the letter. What can you do? Will they forward the letter to you? How will you get the money? The check is made out to the "Ottoman Bank." You will probably get the money. I'll order them to transfer it to Palestine. I hope I'll be able to send you more. Believe me, I don't lack goodwill. If only we can do it.

In spring 1938, we arrived in Haifa, where relatives were waiting for us on the shore. I immediately hated Eretz-Israel and missed Moscow. For me, Palestine was another way station in my life, after Warsaw, Moscow, and Istanbul. I was sure that after a few days we would go on to America.

"Mother, when will we finally get to America, to Father?" I'd ask.

"Why go to him, son? He'll come to us here in Palestine."

"But Mother, I don't like Palestine."

To this day, I can't imagine what made me hate this strip of land at first sight. I refused to learn the language; I hated the blazing sun that blinded my eyes and tanned my fair skin. I fought with the children in the street and in school, and at night I dreamed of my father.

Apparently, Mother was convinced that my father would come to Israel. In that first letter, he wrote:

> About my coming to Palestine? That's my dream. After all, you know I'm a great supporter of Palestine and the Hebrew language. I hope that at the first opportunity (that is, when I've saved up enough money to pay for the trip), I'll crawl onto a ship and have a good time swimming to Tel Aviv.
>
> . . . Write me about everything in detail. How you are living and what are you doing in Palestine? Palestine is a free country, and you can write whatever you want from there. Palestine isn't under Stalin's rule, where people walk around scared 24 hours a day. If I were in Russia, 24 hours a day wouldn't be enough. I would be in dread 48 hours a day, not a moment less. Let them go to hell with their "socialism." I believe that there's more

socialism in the kibbutzim of Palestine than in all of
Russia.

The next day we went to Grandmother's house on Brenner
Street in Tel Aviv. This was a rickety old house with cracked
walls. Grandmother Bayla lived in a two-room apartment that
smelled of musty holy books. The shelves were filled with sacred
items: silver chalices, a Hanukkah lamp, candlesticks, tattered
Bibles and prayer books. A tenant occupied one of the rooms,
and we had to share a room with her. To my delight, I discovered
a small citrus grove in the courtyard of the apartment building;
I hurried down and soon climbed to the top of a tree, where I
spent most of the day with my daydreams and memories. I
fantasized that I had escaped from Palestine, gone back to Warsaw, and from there to the vacation town of Szwider, where we
used to spend the summer. For whole days, I would sit in the
tree, and my mother even brought me my meals there.

"Gigi, I can't climb up so high," pleaded my mother.

"It's really easy, Mother. See that big branch? Put one foot
here and the other foot on that branch."

"But I'm holding a bowl of soup!"

Years later, my father told me that, in his youth, he had read
forbidden books in a tree; it was from that high station that he
encountered Schopenhauer, Nietzsche, Hegel, and Knut Hamsun. "A tree was for me a refuge from orthodox society and has
symbolized that ever since. That was the place where I met the
great classicists I still quote," he said when I described my first
days in Eretz-Israel to him.

Grandmother decided that her grandson would have the
religious education appropriate for the scion of a rabbinical
dynasty. My mother the communist, for whom religion had
represented "the opiate of the masses," didn't resist. After her

intellectual world collapsed around her, she no longer cared
about my education. I was enrolled in the Moriah Gymnasium
on Bogroshov Street in Tel Aviv. I had to wear a black skullcap
and pray every morning with the other children in the school
synagogue. The transition was too abrupt. In Turkey I hadn't
gone to school because we were there illegally, and suddenly
here I had to mumble incomprehensible words and sway back
and forth. From the very first day I hated that school. I had only
attended kindergarten in Moscow, and I had never learned how
to study. Having to obey teachers was entirely new to me. I
refused to learn Hebrew, and the other children learned Polish,
Russian, and Turkish words from me.

"Mother, let's go back to Moscow," I pleaded after my first
day at school.

"Gigi, we can never go back to Moscow. We were expelled
from there," she answered bitterly.

I was put in the third grade, isolated from everyone by
language. I sat in class all day catching flies and tying threads to
their legs; when they attempted to fly, the class cheered loudly.
The teacher didn't know what to do with me. My mother was
summoned to the principal's office, but it was my grandmother
who came instead and explained that I was the descendant of a
distinguished rabbinical dynasty. "He'll be a great scholar," she
declared.

Next to the classroom was a closet with writing materials.
One day, a fly tied with thread landed on the teacher's book. He
locked me in the closet and furiously pummeled my shoulders,
paralyzing both my arms. I didn't cry. Crying meant asking for
mercy, and I refused to do that. When he finished, I was taken
out of the closet and almost fainted. Mr. Freund, the teacher,
was sure that he had taught me a lesson. I didn't tell my mother
about the incident.

The only good thing about that gymnasium were the eucalyptus trees, with thick trunks and dense branches, around Bogroshov Square across the street. When Mr. Freund realized that hitting me didn't work, his first words on entering the classroom each day were: "Good morning, children. Singer, get out!" So I spent more time in the trees than in class. Sitting at the top of the eucalyptus, I would talk to my father and tell him about Mr. Freund, begging him to come beat up the teacher.

One day, however, I found a way to stop the blows. I was in the tree as usual late one afternoon, after the other students had gone home for the day, when I saw Mr. Freund and a woman making their way to the bench that was situated directly underneath where I was sitting. I looked down on them. Mr. Freund glanced all around and, not seeing anyone, slipped his hand under the woman's dress, and the two of them started kissing. I couldn't help sticking two fingers in my mouth and whistling in admiration, shouting in Hebrew: "Mr. Freund, if you hit me again tomorrow, the whole class is gonna know what you're doing!" That was the first Hebrew sentence that came out of my mouth.

They leaped to their feet in a panic and took off. From that day on, there were no more blows. At the end of the year, my mother was called in to see the principal, who told her that in his opinion I was ready to be promoted to a higher grade — but not in his school.

Years later, as we sat in Steinberg's, I told my father that story. He looked at me lovingly and said: "Son, all the suffering and grief you experienced in your youth is wonderful material for literature. Believe me, if I had come to Palestine in those days, I would have given that Mr. Freund a good thrashing."

I glanced at his fragile body and delicate hands and smiled. He couldn't even have tied a piece of thread to the back legs of a fly.

8

DELICATE RELATIONS

Relations between my father and mother went from bad to worse. My mother claimed that when they lived in Warsaw, my father rented rooms so he could write without being disturbed, but according to her, it was mostly so he could bring women there. She had proof of it, she said. When she first got pregnant, he insisted that she have an abortion; but as a rabbi's daughter she couldn't do such a thing, and she firmly refused. My father, in a moment of despair, suggested that they commit suicide together by throwing themselves under the trolley. He could not tolerate the idea of having a kid in his house.

"Do you remember proposing such a thing?" I asked him later.

"No, I don't, but it's possible. Your mother's memory is better than mine, but that's not important anymore. I know I was never a devoted and loving father. My weakness is that, in my soul, I'm still a bachelor. I soon understood that the whole thing was one big mistake, but I didn't know how to get out of the trap I had fallen into. I wandered around the streets of Warsaw for days, escaping from your mother, from you, from myself, running to other women — most of them show up in my stories. I was trying to repress the fact that I had a son, but I didn't have much success."

"I think you did," I said ruefully.

He glanced at me and smiled sadly.

I asked him why he didn't have children with Alma. After all, he was thirty-six when he married her, and she was a few years younger. He replied that Alma had wanted children very much, but he was staunchly opposed to it.

"My stories are my children," he said. "Alma's got two children from her previous marriage, and I've got one son. Isn't that enough? Children are a burden. See, you came to New York, and even though I'm glad we met, it was crowded. I was really relieved when you found work and left. Don't get me wrong, I'm loyal to you as every father is to his son. But on condition that nothing gets in the way of my writing. Fortunately, you understood that."

He picked up a letter I had written to my daughter, looked at the handwriting with a surprised expression: "Sometimes I look at you, your face, and somehow I find myself in you. You're more like me than you are like your mother. Even your handwriting is almost the same as mine, even though you grew up far away from me."

And again he seemed to feel a need to talk about my mother. She was the complete opposite of him. He was a confirmed individualist, a recluse, and she was very social. Their apartment was always filled with people at all hours of the day: her friends carried on political arguments there. If he happened to come home in the middle of the day, he would find himself out of place and would run off to the Writers' Club. My father lived like a nomad. He never ignored me, he insisted, but the money he brought home wasn't enough. He kept accusing my mother of using his money to finance the printing of her leaflets and other communist propaganda.

"We fought and made up constantly until she was arrested." He was terribly ashamed of having been imprisoned for even one day. That news appeared in the Yiddish newspaper, and it made it worse for him. Two versions of his imprisonment appeared in his memoirs in *The Forward*. In an article in 1956, he said that he had not been imprisoned but had just been summoned to an interrogation and asked what he knew about Dora's political activities. (Dora was my mother's underground pseudonym.)

"I wanted to help her and not lie, so I said: 'The only thing I know is that her mind is all confused.'"

According to that article, the investigator was satisfied with his answer and released him. In 1956, people in the United States were still intimidated by the specter of McCarthyism, so he apparently preferred not to disclose his imprisonment, especially since it concerned alleged communist activities.

However, a second article in 1964 contains a more detailed version of the event. A detective arrested my father on the street and brought him to jail for an interrogation:

> The walls were smeared with such graffiti as "Fascist Dogs!" "Long Live Communism!" . . . I lay awake almost all night. . . . In the early evening, they brought me into the office where someone who looked like a senior interrogator was sitting. He politely offered me a cigarette, and asked:
> "What's going on with you?"
> "That's what I'm asking you. Everybody knows I'm not a communist."
> "But you live with a communist."

These passages are clear indications of the complicated relations between my father and mother. Three years later, he left us and went to America.

When I sailed to America twenty years later to meet my father, I decided I would not settle past accounts with him. I wanted to accept him as he was, despite my mother's accusations. She didn't want me to go and tried to persuade me to give up the visit, fearing that I would suffer bitter disappointment. I didn't pay any attention to her advice; I was eager to meet my father. For twenty years I had constructed a father in my imagination, and I wanted to close the circle. I was convinced that after such a long separation, the fire of love between father and son was certainly extinguished, and it was pointless to try to revive it. I came to him with low expectations from the start. If my father and I could just come to some understanding, that would be good enough.

It took me a long time to understand how complicated my parents' relations had been. My father's hasty departure for America and his promises to reunite the family there when his economic situation improved were, it turned out, nothing but empty words, to which we clung in vain. Five years after my father's arrival in America, he married Alma. He never wrote to us about it. Why had he concealed his marriage to Alma? I asked him, and he simply shrugged his shoulders. The answer was the same — in his soul he always felt that he had remained a bachelor. His letters, however, indicate that until he met Alma, he was consumed by regret. This is from a letter he wrote to my mother in 1938:

> What wouldn't I give to be in Palestine now and to see you and dear Gigi whom I love so much and miss so much. I hope I won't have to wait as long as I've waited so far. I'm deeply convinced that I'll soon be able to "drop in on" you and talk about everything.
>   The years we've been apart — three and a half years — naturally take their toll. I will always remem-

ber you whatever happens — I can't deny that we
spent years together in joy and fights, in various
strange circumstances, which only the two of us know.
I miss you and I'm sometimes forced to think about
how close we were. Even if I live a thousand years, I
can't forget our apartment at 57 Leszno Street, which I
see as clearly in my mind's eye as if I had left it only
yesterday, with the bed and everything, everything. I
also have to remember the harsh quarrels from the day
we met to the day we parted. I can't and I won't judge
which of us was guilty of that. I believe all the guilt
comes from our radically different natures. But in spite
of everything — ignoring the contradiction — I do
miss you and the child. I miss the caresses and the
games, but I wouldn't want to go through it all again,
all the quarrels, all the anger, all the escapes from
home, and all the other troubles I went through in
those days. When I look at our past I see a lot of delicacy and a lot of happy moments, but not a single sign
of peace and quiet. In a certain sense, we need to get to
know each other again. If the same conflicts and the
same troubles are still waiting for me in the future, I
don't want to go back to it all, even though I yearn for
you and the dear child and everything that was. What
is meaningful at twenty becomes completely devoid
of meaning at thirty, not to mention forty. I am now
thirty-four and you are of course three years younger.
It's hard to believe that we're already in our thirties.

Love and regret on the one hand, and reservations and with-
drawal on the other. These contradictions appear in his letters
up to the time of his marriage to Alma in 1940.

My father and I were eating breakfast in a New York restaurant. I remember ordering an omelet but not being as hungry as I thought, and I left part of it on my plate. My father was furious. "Why don't you finish the omelet?" He took a slice of bread, mopped up what was left, and ate it.

"You sold a story to *The New Yorker* for three thousand dollars this week. Can't you afford to order another omelet, which costs about a quarter?" I asked.

"I can't see food go to waste."

Was he compulsively stingy? Absolutely not, he replied. But he did have trouble adjusting to his life of recent comfort after so many years of financial straits, when he literally didn't have a cent in his pocket and had to calculate everything very carefully. He suffered years of austerity and literary muteness when he first arrived in this foreign country. He had taken refuge in a foreign language and in a society where he felt terribly lost. *Lost in America* is the title of one of the autobiographical books describing his first years in this country. He told me that in his early American years, he often thought of committing suicide.

In that same letter to my mother, he expressed his frustration:

> Here, in America, I am suffering a hard breakdown. First of all, I carry on a relentless battle literally with poverty and hunger. Second, I practically don't work. For me and my literary plans, America is a cold shower. The Yiddish world here is poor, small, a thousand times more wretched than in Warsaw. I've simply lost all desire to work — I couldn't bear the dark "realism" that prevails here in life in general. I write "realism" in quotation marks because, in fact, it has nothing really to do with realism. I try to take pen in hand, but I put it down immediately.

From the beginning of their life together, my father and Alma kept separate bank accounts. Alma was afflicted with "shopping sickness," my father claimed, and wasted most of the money she earned buying things. "If you woke Alma up in the middle of the night and told her that there was a shoe sale in the Bronx, she'd jump out of bed, willing to leave at once for a shopping spree. Shopping is her great passion. Every morning she gets to work early at Lord and Taylor as if she were going to a party." My father, in contrast, was afraid to go into stores for fear that they would cheat him. Alma always bought his clothes and brought them home for him to try on.

"And what happens to a Yiddish writer who gets rich?" I asked as we were drinking coffee.

"What happens? Nothing. How many meals a day do you think a rich man can eat? Vegetarians don't have many delicacies. I usually eat a potato, vegetable soup, spinach blintzes, and a little kasha. For that you don't need to be a millionaire. Eating isn't one of my great passions. And what does a man like me need? If, God forbid, I was locked up in prison for some reason, I'd be happy if the guards would just give me paper and something to write with. Believe me, I could be very happy there without radio and television."

"And what about women?"

"Right. I do have a need to love and be loved. But aside from that, I don't need anything. You've lived in my house and seen me put on that faded gray bathrobe every morning, the one I bought forty years ago, the same shabby house slippers, sitting on my regular chair, with my notebook on my knee, writing."

My father became rich over the years. He published many books, all successful. He became a popular lecturer and made a lot of money. But he never gave up his old habits.

9

SOBERING UP

In February 1956, the Twentieth Communist Party Congress convened in Moscow for the first time since Stalin's death in 1953. At a closed meeting, the leader of the Soviet Union, Nikita Khrushchev, condemned the crimes of Stalin and his followers in a speech that was subsequently smuggled to the West and printed in the *New York Times*. I read it a few times in disbelief. One of the things Khrushchev mentioned in his speech was the proposal in Lenin's will to transfer Stalin from the position of party secretary. Khrushchev accused Stalin of putting thousands of loyal and innocent communists to death. He told of Stalin's drastic measures before World War II and how confused he had been in the early stages of the war. As a young idealist and communist, I was shattered by the list of Stalin's crimes.

Had they really been deceiving us all those years? I asked myself. Could Stalin have been one of the greatest criminals humanity has known? I handed the newspaper to my father, who read it slowly, shaking his head in disbelief. He remained silent. I was grateful to him for not saying a spiteful "I told you so." He must have sensed my agony and decided not to rub salt in my wounds. Days went by, and as if by some silent, tacit agreement, we never discussed it.

One day he phoned me at work and said softly: "Son, I know very well what you're going through. I grew up in Poland among writers and poets whose lives were ended under the Nazis. Siberia was no different. Millions froze to death there on the altar of communism. The dictatorship of the proletariat is a recipe for terror, corruption, and murder."

I didn't reply. In previous conversations, whenever he criticized the Soviet regime, he would get emotional responses from me. This time he spoke gently, as if he shared my grief. For three years, Stalin's picture had hung in my room on the kibbutz. I had sincerely believed that Stalin was realizing socialism in his country, just as we were on the kibbutz. Without the Soviet Union, the kibbutz couldn't fill its historic destiny as the avant-garde of the workers building a new society in Eretz-Israel. Now Khrushchev came along and depicted Stalin as a brutal, selfish, suspicious tyrant with a mad lust for power. How could the kibbutz survive as an isolated socialist cell if it had all been a lie? For us, the Soviet Union wasn't only a faith, it was a source of inspiration, a deep emotional identification, a kind of "second homeland." I tried to explain that to my father.

"What?! The Soviet Union as a second homeland for Jews?!" he shouted. A long silence set in between us. I could hear his excited breathing through the phone.

"Let me tell you something that may help you understand what Russia meant to us," I said. "When we were high school students, the Bible teacher wanted us to learn chapters from the Song of Songs that weren't part of the curriculum. 'This is a marvelous poem,' he told us. 'If you want us to learn a wonderful poem,' we told him, 'teach us the poetry of Mayakovsky.' We all deeply believed that the 'new man' was being created in the Soviet Union."

"New man? A useless cliché! The regime hasn't yet been

born that can create a new man. Only the Holy-One-Blessed-Be-He can do that." He was silent a moment and then added: "Son, don't be melancholic. You were sick with communism, a disease that afflicted untold millions, including your mother. I'm not sure that Khrushchev will rule less cruelly than Stalin."

That same year, in October, I heard on the radio about the arrival in New York of a ship of refugees from Hungary. They had fled after the Hungarian revolt against their government and the brutal intervention of the Soviet Union that followed. The newspapers had described the Soviet suppression of the revolt in blood and fire. I was skeptical of the reports, as usual, but decided nonetheless to go to the piers to see for myself. Near the pier, a man newly arrived in a wrinkled suit stood in front of a large crowd and introduced himself as a member of the "Central Committee of the Communist party in Budapest." He was telling them all about the Red Army soldiers who had crushed loyal communists with a column of tanks. He told about the secretary of a suburban branch of the party whose tongue had been torn out for having refused to denounce his comrades. I was terribly shaken and called my father to tell him what I had seen and heard.

"Stalin is a murderer. It's high time you sober up. That regime is rotten."

I didn't answer.

My spiritual world was crumbling. What had happened to Mother Russia, the country that I had so idealized for the past twenty years? Where were the good Russians of *Quiet Flows the Don*? Of *Panfilov's Men*? What about the Russian people? And the kibbutz? I wondered how the members were reacting upon learning about these revelations. How is the party newspaper addressing that? What about our leaders? I recalled one veteran member of our kibbutz who had been a representative of the movement in Europe. When the war ended, he made an extensive tour of Eastern Europe and the Soviet Union. In the various communist countries, he met refugees from the Holocaust, members of the Politburo, communist leaders; and he heard hair-raising stories about Stalin's dreadful regime. He was also told about the violence of the Ukrainian Red Army soldiers and their anti-Semitism. When that man returned to Eretz-Israel, he closeted himself with the leaders of the movement for an entire day, reporting to them in great detail on that "Russian socialism." In total shock, they insisted that he not tell the members, claiming that "the movement wasn't mature enough to change its sympathetic relation to the Soviet Union." They were also convinced that "one couldn't judge a regime during a war." In my own kind of denial, I justified the decision not to participate in the anti-Soviet propaganda spread by the Holocaust survivors as they immigrated to Eretz-Israel. Agreeing with my father's unequivocal conclusion that "Stalin was a murderer" would have been the end of my faith in socialism. I wasn't ready for that yet. Nor was I mature enough to change the way I felt about the Soviet Union.

We walked to Broadway. A fire truck dashing by deafened us with the sound of its siren along Central Park. Young blacks ran by us, shouting. An alley cat rubbed up against a lamppost and whined in despair while two enormous wolfhounds stood on either side of the sidewalk, blocking the cat's way and barking furiously. New York, all of a sudden, seemed like a jungle to me.

We finally reached Broadway as it started raining. The fruit stand owners were hurrying to cover the produce with plastic sheets.

"Seems that God takes care of His business very successfully, with or without Stalin," declared my father, surveying the street as he held on to his hat so it wouldn't fly off in the wind.

"Don't get carried away. God doesn't have any status on Broadway," I replied.

"So who do you think controls the traffic here?"

"The traffic lights."

"And who created the traffic lights?"

"Man."

"And who created man?"

"And who created God?"

10

THIEF OF LOVE

Each time my father visited Israel, he would bring me one of his new stories. I would translate it into Hebrew, and we would sit for hours together, polishing every sentence. I was surprised at his mastery of Hebrew. He remembered it rather well, I thought, given the fact that he hadn't used it for years. He came about twice a year and would stay at a hotel in Tel Aviv or Haifa. My father had a lot of friends in Israel — writers and poets from Warsaw or Bilgoray — and he enjoyed seeing them. Human landscapes enriched his writing, he kept saying.

I recall one day, at the kibbutz, receiving a call from someone telling me that my father was in Israel. I was used to never being informed in advance of his arrival. The following day I went to his hotel and found him sitting next to the window, across from a heavyset woman who was murmuring syllables with her eyes closed. It was Margot Klausner, director of the Herziliya Studios; both her hands were on his bald head, and both his hands were on her bosom. The fragmentary syllables turned into words, and she spoke in the sepulchral tones of a medium:

"You, writer Isaac Bashevis Singer, must grant me the film rights to all your books and stories. Yes, you must do that now,"

she repeated very slowly, sometimes in a whisper and sometimes with a tremor, like a magician evoking spirits.

When my father saw me, he took his hands off her chest and
nodded a greeting, and the performance continued. Mrs.
Klausner would stop now and then as if she were waiting for
more messages from the spirit world, and then my father would
glance at me with an apologetic smile, as if to say: What do you
say about that, eh?

All of a sudden, Margot Klausner opened her eyes, saw me,
and quickly took her hands off his head. She nodded a greeting
and, changing to a matter-of-fact tone, said: "Mr. Singer, I've
had documents drawn up by an attorney, and all you've got to
do is sign them. You heard the command of the higher powers
with your own ears."

She pulled a bunch of documents out of her purse and
showed him where to sign. My father glanced at the documents, raised his reddish eyebrows, wrinkled his smooth forehead, and said: "Even though the higher powers command it, I
can't sign right now."

"What do you mean, right now?" She was angry. Ignoring
her question, he went back to scanning the documents. From
time to time he would shake his head and talk to himself:
"*Gimpel the Fool* and *The Slave* and *The Estate* and *The Manor*,
and even the story 'The Bishop's Robe.' "

" 'The Bishop's Robe' is my favorite story," exclaimed Margot Klausner, her eyes flashing. "As soon as I read it, I knew you
were writing about me. The higher forces dictated the story to
you. I'm Bessie Feingevirtz and Phyllis Gurdin."

Then she opened her mouth and began emitting strange
noises from that story: "charopakitcichi, hatchomarumbi, lep-
tchocalduku," and other weird words. Her body swayed from
side to side, her eyes rolled wildly, and foam appeared at the

corners of her mouth. My father raised his eyebrows and looked amused. Her chest was heaving as if she had just finished running a marathon. My father held on to the documents and became pensive — trapped between the command of the higher powers and his reluctance to release his property rights. After a while, he finally said: "It's not nice to argue in front of my son."

Margot looked daggers at me. Her deal was ruined.

He walked her to the door, telling her how much he had enjoyed her company, and invited her to come see him again. As for the film rights, he added, "We'll talk about it some more. I'm not running away," leaving her a shred of hope.

"Had you signed, she would have made a fortune," I told him after she had left.

"She's a bad medium. You shouldn't mix business with higher powers," he concluded.

"Why didn't you tell her to go to hell?"

"She was already there. And anyway, I really hate hurting women's feelings."

All the women in my father's life suffered very much from his tendency to always leave a trace of hope when there wasn't any justification for it. He even promised to marry some of them. More often than not, and because of unkept promises, he got himself entangled in situations he had great trouble getting out of. The solution was always the same — escape. That same pattern had applied when he left my mother and immigrated to the United States, promising to bring us over as soon as his situation improved. And like all the other women before and after her, my mother had believed him and waited twelve years before marrying again. He, on the other hand, married Alma five years after he came to America.

"Did you really intend to give Margot Klausner the film rights to your works?" I asked my father.

"Of course not."

"But you made her think you were courting her," I remarked.

"I never courted a woman in my life. By nature I'm very shy," he explained. According to my father, the women always came after him, and he couldn't help being swept away by them. Except in his works, his real battlefield, he simply could not take a firm position with women. "In my writing I fight furiously with men, women, and even demons and spirits. By nature, I'm a passive character who has a hard time making bold decisions." In life, he couldn't say no to women. In *The Magician of Lublin,* my father created a strong hero, Yasha Mauser, who takes his fate into his own hands and who, at the end of his life, flees into an isolated cell, "the little prison," as his wife Esther puts it. In his writing, my father often constructed a kind of abstract jail for some of his characters.

"Things are determined, and we don't have any control over them. In some sense, Herman of *Enemies, a Love Story* represents my true nature, and Yasha Mauser is what I aspire to be."

Although I often heard his female admirers say how "wonderful" my father was, that "wonderfulness" led to disillusion and bitter disappointment for them. His weakness was women. He frequently reminded us that he had to love and had to be loved. Almost every afternoon he was in Steinberg's restaurant with a woman, and it always amused me to see how he "introduced" them.

Until he received the Nobel Prize, my father was listed in the Manhattan telephone directory. Anyone who wished to call him could and did. A great many women admired his writing,

and some would call him about stories that they were sure
would be of interest to him. If the woman's voice or the story
sounded interesting, my father would invite her to join him at
Steinberg's (later, at the American Restaurant). Many of my
father's stories are faithful representations that emanate from
those encounters.

For years he lectured at universities and Jewish centers in
various places, and he was often accompanied to his hotel after
the lecture by an admiring female student. He would enjoy
entertaining his young guest with an unending flow of bons
mots. Sometimes she'd end up spending the night. My father
received dozens of fan letters every day. Occasionally he would
single out a letter — wondering what character might be lurking behind this "curlicued writing." He would take the trouble
to call and invite the author of the letter to lunch. He had, of
course, no idea who she would turn out to be, and he always
wondered whether there would be any connection between
her pleasant voice on the telephone and her appearance. "Yes,
I'm an actor who needs an audience, or at least one female
admirer. Women, you know, are marvelous listeners. As long as
the man is restrained and polite, the woman is all ears. She
inhales his words, responds excitedly, waves of admiration wash
over her. Women are a splendid audience," he would always say.

I concluded that my father was a Jewish Casanova. An example taken from one of his books:

> I managed to do this with Gina. The more drawn she
> grew to me, the more drawn was I to others. Al-
> though I felt no love toward her (who knows what
> love is anyway), I started up with the maid at the house
> where I boarded. Marila and I had already kissed
> and made clandestine plans for me to come to her

bed when the household was asleep. I had also promised to go through with the wedding ceremony with
Miss Stefa, an act which Gina would consider treach-
ery. . . . I had become a thief not of money but of
love. I had discovered how easy it was to inveigle
oneself into a woman's heart.

I'm not sure that every tale reached a sexual climax. Sometimes, he once told me, he completed in writing what he
wanted to realize in reality.

In Warsaw, he moved from room to room and from apartment to apartment; and — if his stories are to be believed — in
many cases the landlady or her daughter shared her bed with
him. Even long after he met my mother, his habits didn't
change. Every other woman became like a life raft saving him
from his failed marriage.

In 1938, my father wrote to my mother:

> Yes, you write about a dream you had that I am living
> here with Esther. That's really funny. Ever since I left,
> I haven't written to Esther. As far as I'm concerned,
> my relations with her were the stupidest thing I ever
> did. After her, I made a lot of mistakes like that. I had
> a lot of beautiful and elegant women. From that
> point of view, I'm a great success, as they say in
> America. But I never stopped missing you and I
> never understood why we got mad and sneered at
> each other. There's one thing you hold on to: my
> past, my youth, my child.

In his first years in America, and before meeting Alma, my
father's letters to my mother were full of regrets. He was alone,

estranged from his surroundings, and his letters were nostalgic
about the things and people of the past. But that didn't last. A
long silence followed.

I was often asked about the secret of my father's success with
women. I must say, it intrigued me as well. In 1985, I remember
being surprised and a little amused when *McCall's* magazine
chose him as one of the ten sexiest men in America. The author
of the article wrote that, in my father's case, his success had not
so much to do with his looks or his body but with his ability to
charm women with his conversation. "There's an enormous
energy dammed up in him which is capable of sending a rocket
to the moon. Women are generally attracted to movie stars or
to theater actors, while conversations with him leave women
with a yearning to meet again. He describes such strong lust
that the page catches fire as you read it."

My father was always very open in his conversations with
women and never hesitated to tell them intimate details of his
life. They often felt encouraged to tell him their secrets. He
would listen sensitively, which explained to me why women
trusted him. According to my father, when married women
slept with him, they didn't feel guilty. He mentioned to me
with pride the one who told him: "I felt marvelous. A real
catharsis!" My father considered "the bed as the continuation of
the conversation, but horizontally." Curiosity and sincerity
often seemed to sweep him off to shores he hadn't planned to
visit and from which, in some instances, it was hard to sail back
home.

Alma chose to ignore his exploits. A great writer also has
weaknesses, she kept saying. As long as things didn't get out of
hand, she tolerated his straying. It amused me to watch him
time and again decide whether or not to hang up on some
woman caller; there were times I would hear his voice become

as soft as a child's and promptly ask when they could meet. His constant curiosity and his desire to know a woman's soul caused him to get sucked into the whirlpools of many women's lives. Threats of suicide on the part of some of his women admirers often prevented him from breaking contact, long after the affair was over.

There were two women who seemed to have had relations with my father for some time. The first was Dova Gruber, whom I met in Steinberg's. Her hair-raising tales of the Holocaust were incorporated in part into my father's stories of Masha and Tamara in *Enemies, a Love Story*. Dova worked as his Yiddish secretary and even traveled abroad with him. In the summer of 1975, my father was invited to receive an honorary doctorate at the Hebrew University. He traveled to Israel with Dova, and they stayed together at the Park Hotel in Tel Aviv. I remember that the three of us were sitting and talking in his room when, unannounced, Alma suddenly appeared. My father blushed, and Dova turned pale.

"Alma, what are you doing here?" he asked, fearful and annoyed.

"I came for the ceremony," she answered calmly.

I admired Alma's courage. She had decided that the affair with Dova had gone too far. As I sat at the ceremony with Dova, in one of the upper rows of the amphitheater on Mount Scopus, I could see that Dova had tears in her eyes.

"He promised to marry me dozens of times, and there they are sitting in front with the dignitaries, while you and I are way up here with the nobodies."

"Dova, he promised to divorce Alma and marry you just as he promised Esther and Stefa and Sabina in Poland, and God knows how many other women in America," I said to her, hoping to bring some sense to her broken heart.

Alma Singer, formerly Wasserman, grew up in an assimilated German Jewish family. She met my father at a resort near New York and left her husband for him, giving up a life of luxury to live in a tiny apartment with an unknown author who wrote in a language she didn't understand. She apparently had to support him for years. Alma started out as a saleswoman at Lord and Taylor and was promoted to a senior position. She got up early every day and took the subway downtown to work. According to my father, she spent her whole salary on shopping but never touched his money. A journalist once asked her what she saw in my father. She replied: "He's a genuine writer who can't fix himself a meal or wash dishes or do the shopping. He's got no idea of business, even when it has to do with publishing his own books."

She had tried her hand at writing, she told the journalist, but hadn't dared show it to her husband. She was occasionally invited to lecture on his work and was active in the Humane Society.

The other long-term woman in my father's life was Dvora Menashe, who had met him when he was invited to give a lecture at Bard. She had seen an ad on the university bulletin board for a volunteer to drive my father back to the city after his lecture. She volunteered, and that was how they met. She worked with him for years, helping him type his books and stories, and they became close. When Alma's health failed in the 1980s, Dvora Menashe became a friend of the family, helping with shopping and various errands and making their lives easier. In my father's last year, she even went down to Miami to visit them. Decades younger than my father, Dvora Menashe is married to a rabbi. Apparently there was no issue of marriage between them, or if there was, my father didn't tell me about it.

So, in the end, it was Alma who emerged victorious in the

struggle for my father's soul. In his final years, he was all hers;
and when he fell ill, she took care of him devotedly, lovingly,
and loyally, to his last day. I often asked him if all his adventures
had been worth the trouble they got him into. "I'm Herman,
for good and for bad." He smiled, shrugging his shoulders.
"Does a man have control over his lust? Life is an overflowing
sea. Every affair enriched my life and my creativity. No, I'm not
sorry. I'm a bachelor, a bachelor in my soul. Even if I married a
whole harem of women, I'd still act like a bachelor. Every
woman who passes by on Broadway is a riddle to me. I'd like to
stop her in the street and ask: 'Excuse me, ma'am, where are
you from? Do you believe in God? In free choice? In reincarna-
tion? What are your relations with your husband?' I've got an
ability to decipher the dots of pain in their lives. My stories get
their shape not only from the terrific landscapes I describe but
mainly from real characters, mostly from women."

When I read *The Slave,* I told my father how deeply impressed I was by his descriptions of the Carpathian Mountains,
where Jacob Bzik's cowherd was brought: "He threw open the
barn door and saw the mountaintops stretching into the distance. Some of the peaks, their slopes overgrown with forests,
seemed close at hand, giants with green beards. Mist rising from
the woods like tenuous curls made Jacob think of Samson."

"Were you ever in the Carpathian Mountains?" I asked my
father.

He laughed, pleased at my being able to recite the passage
from memory. "All landscapes are here in my head." He pointed
to his forehead. "I don't have to go anywhere. Travel exhausts
me. You can see the Carpathian Mountains from here, from my
window in Manhattan. In my writing, everything is lust, even
landscapes. Philosophers in the past tried to neutralize feelings
and lust, and to ground their thoughts in logic, assuming that

everything goes through our brain. Take away our lust and it
looks like lettuce leaves. I believe in feelings that turned into lust.
I believe that when a man and a woman kiss and declare that they
can't live without each other — that's the start of a spiritual
matter, not just a material one. Our world is so mysterious. You
leave your house, meet a woman on Broadway, and your life
changes. By the way, what time is it?"

"One thirty."

"I've got to go. A woman called me from the Bronx yesterday and swore to me by all that's holy that, in a cafeteria on
Jerome Avenue, she saw Adolf Hitler. Strange, isn't it? I've got
to hear her story."

"Nonsense. Can it be true?"

"My son, everything can be true in the complicated world of
the Holy-One-Blessed-Be-He. Hitler can live in the Bronx
and show up in a cafeteria on Jerome Avenue."

11

SILENT YODEL

During one of my father's visits to Israel, I went to see him in Haifa, at the Dan Carmel Hotel. We talked about translations, and I asked him why he had suggested that I translate his books into Hebrew when he knew I wasn't an experienced translator. He looked out the window at the top of the Carmel toward the golden dome of the Bahai Temple, pondered a moment, and said: "I really did hesitate quite a bit. I was afraid, for instance, that if your translations turned out to be awful, the whole thing might damage our relationship." He emphasized that, when it came to literature, he was neither tolerant nor compromising. He knew Hebrew well enough to detect mistakes or imprecisions. He recalled that he had worried how I would respond if he were to tell me that I wasn't fit for that work. "I knew you didn't know Yiddish very well, and I did hesitate; then I decided that that could even be an advantage, because I would go over the work, correct its style, and change its content. I hoped we'd get closer to each other through our translations, and that I'd get to know you better. My circle of friends are mostly publishers, translators, literary agents, people connected with my work in some way. I don't have time for other people. Of course, there are also a few people from my hometown of Bilgoray, and some lady friends I've made over the years."

"Is a close relationship between us so important to you?" I couldn't help asking.

"Oh yes, very important," he replied.

"You know, when I came to your house in New York in 1955, you made it clear that you didn't have any time for me. You didn't even bother to ask me if I had enough money for lunch when I wandered around the city. You may not believe it, but I was often hungry in those days. What kind of a father were you?"

"A terrible father. Even today I'm still not a model father. But if you didn't have any money in your pocket, why didn't you ask me for some?"

"Why didn't it occur to you to offer me some? You had brought a son to you in America from far away, one who had been a stranger to you for twenty years. Once in your house you ignored him. I couldn't ask you for money. If my father doesn't offer me money, it means he doesn't feel close to me or doesn't feel a need to give, I told myself. Occasionally you'd take a dollar bill out of your pocket, assuming that it was enough to pay for my food, my subway, the bus, and everything else. Couldn't you have afforded to be a little more generous? My disappointment was such that I almost returned to Israel."

He looked at me surprised, with a sad expression on his face. His hands moved restlessly. "Oh, hearing you now, I realize that I didn't act right, and I'm sorry. It's hard for me to explain my behavior. I never had to share my expenses. Looking at you at the time reminded me of your mother, who always asked me for money. And in general, our relations were spoiled."

In 1941, after his marriage to Alma, my father wrote to my mother:

We have been separated for almost six years and for people like us that is quite a long time. Both of us have had various conflicts by now — and you can't turn back the clock. That doesn't mean that you've become a stranger to me. The years when we shared joys and sorrows — those years do exist and can't be repressed from my memory. The dear son, who certainly regards his father as a traitor, is the direct result of our life in common. We don't want any more children. He was and will remain my "only son." . . . My private life and my personal nonsense have nothing to do with him. . . . A father is a father, even when he's not such a serious provider.

. . . You write in your letter that I deserted you. But you did the same thing to me. You went away from me never to return. . . . I believe that you will get married and I hope you'll get a better man than me. What we have in common is our past. . . . Different things have happened to me. I've remained the same person. . . . In truth, to this very day I don't know what love is. I've got a strange feeling: I can be loved in the past as well as in the present. Those aren't phrases. I think there's a kind of reward for such "generous hearts." Let it remain between us. We — I hope — will see each other again someday and talk about everything, about the problems I've raised here.

And in that same letter, my father seems to sum up his relationship with my mother:

I don't think there's any point going over the past again and again. Such things happen to thousands

and millions. . . . May Hitler have a strange death and
then the road to Eretz-Israel will be closer.

That day in Haifa, as we confronted one of our many emotional topics, my father looked at me and said: "When I think
now of your first days in America, it's hard for me to explain
why I didn't provide you with pocket money, considering that I
too had had hard times when I arrived in that country."

"Maybe you're just stingy?" I suggested.

"Me, stingy!" He closed his eyes for a while and clenched his
lips. I had offended him. We remained silent. "The fact is I did
pay for your passage," he said, looking away.

"That was from royalties you probably wouldn't have been
able to get or have access to any other way, given the Israeli laws
at the time," I countered. Our silence lasted a long time.

"Things were hard for me at that time in America. For your
arrival, I had to buy a folding bed and a mattress, and there were
other expenses too. You say I gave you a dollar a day? How did
you manage to come to America and go hungry?" He glanced at
me in astonishment and shook his head sadly. He remembered
that Alma had asked him if he was giving his son money, and he
had replied that of course he was. "How many sons do I have?"

"But you didn't," I said calmly, without anger. "When you
learned that your son found work as a truck driver and could
make his way by himself, you were relieved. He had freed you
from the daily dollar. Let's assume for a moment that I hadn't
found work. What then? Would you still have considered your
son a success? Or a failure? After twenty years of separation, did
you justify your stinginess by the tests you set for him? After a
few days, I had no choice but to go looking for work. I
understood very fast who I was dealing with." Our conversation was turning bitter.

"You know, I hesitated a lot about whether to bring you to America at all," said my father. "I was afraid of all the complications. You would have had to stay in the living room, and all kinds of women would call me up. I'd have to apologize, explain, maybe lie. I consulted with Alma and, to her credit, she insisted that I make up my own mind if I wanted to get to know my son. You ask what would have happened if you hadn't found work. We would have gone back to Israel together after the three weeks I set aside for your visit."

"And the chapter entitled 'Father and Son' would simply have died out," I commented.

He smiled. "The higher forces that run the world apparently thought otherwise. They gave me a successful son and led him to translate my works. I remember that the moment you pulled a hundred dollars out of your pocket, I knew immediately that you were OK, that you wouldn't be a burden to me, that you'd find your way in life, even if you left the kibbutz. I was very happy. For you."

"And for you." I looked up and stared at him. "And maybe your suggestion that I translate your stories into Hebrew was intended, among other things, to save you some money?" Even as I spoke, I was afraid that this time I might seriously offend him.

But he laughed, gave me an amused look, then said: "There may be something to that. Don't forget, I had had several hard years in America. The Jews harshly criticized my writing. I thought that if they'd read me in Israel, maybe that would influence the Jews of America too. Maybe it all does sound like business, but you weren't the only one I enticed into translating my work. I got my nephew Joseph into it too. And my sister's son, Maurice Carr."

"I know. I know that when Maurice Carr helped you with the translation of the play *Yentl,* you were very cruel to him."

We went down to the lobby for coffee, and he suggested that we go on a walk around Mount Carmel. The wind was blowing a whirlpool of dry leaves, gray clouds covered the sky, and children were jumping over the puddles in the gutter. My father stared at the people passing by. "Did it ever occur to you," he said, "that all the people walking on this street are Jews? It's hard for a person like me to get used to that. I usually walk on Broadway, glance at the faces passing by, and try to figure out who is a Jew."

We stopped at a newspaper stand, where, after glancing curiously at the headlines of the Hebrew papers, he asked the vendor if he was sold out of *The Forward*. The man pulled it out of a pile of foreign papers and handed him a copy. My father opened the paper quickly, showing some excitement, and smiled proudly after finding the name: Yitzhak Varshavski, one of his pen names. Before traveling to Israel, he had left four articles with his New York editor, and he was now scanning what he had written. He suddenly grew serious and flushed as he discovered a typographical error. Pulling a pen out of his jacket pocket, he corrected it.

"What did I tell you! Those typesetters are such slobs. They don't understand that a writer doesn't die of heart failure, but of typographical errors," he quoted from one of his stories. Then he went back to our earlier discussion: "You know, before deciding to suggest that you translate my works, I wanted to know what you knew about literature, and I asked if you had read any Tolstoy, Dostoyevsky, Adam Mickiewicz, Knut Hamsun, Kafka. You nodded casually and mentioned the names of the books you'd read. I said to myself, He's a man of the book. Then we played around with Bible quotations. I remembered that you had studied in religious schools, but I was afraid that communism had brainwashed you completely."

"I can still recite passages from *The Communist Manifesto*," I declared.

"I'm sure you can. When you first came to America, you talked in Stalinist clichés. Once we passed a group of striking workers picketing a shop, protesting the owner's unfair treatment of them. A bored policeman, as the law requires, kept them moving. You looked at those workers so sympathetically. In your mind's eye, you surely envisioned a socialist revolution and even discovered the capitalist contradictions of 'an old world to be destroyed root and branch,' as you said. I remember that well. It was in Union Square. Your words then were funny, but frightening too. That was in the fifties, during Joe McCarthy's reign of terror. I was scared that you were going to get me into trouble with your anti-American activities, and I'd be thrown out of that country. I suggested that you go back to Israel at once, and you told me that the kibbutz had decided that you had to stay and help train young people. I didn't like the Ha-Shomer Ha-Tsa'ir movement. It's radical, too close to Stalin. You had even told me that, a month before you came, some FBI agents had been snooping around the New York offices of Ha-Shomer Ha-Tsa'ir. I was very worried."

"At that time, we were close to the Soviet Union, along with many millions of socialists all over the world who believed that good things would come out of the north," I told my father. "But after the Doctors' Trial and Nikita Khrushchev's speech at the Twentieth Congress of the Communist party, we cut ourselves off from the corruption of the Soviet Union. I told you that many times, yet you still persist in identifying me with Stalin. We haven't been part of the revolutionary world for twenty years now."

My father seemed piqued. "You know, the first time I came to Israel, in the summer of 1955, you were in America. I went

to your kibbutz, and your girlfriend at that time, Rivka, arranged for us to sleep in her parents' house. It was a Saturday
night, and after a very good fish dinner, her parents went to the
kibbutz assembly in the dining room, while Alma and I stayed
in their apartment. Alma went to sleep, and I listened to the
radio. I glanced at the bookshelf, which was full of books by
Marx, Engels, Lenin, Stalin, Borokhov. In my naïveté, I had
thought that in a kibbutz of Jewish pioneers I'd find the writings
of Bialik, Shalom Aleichem, S. Y. Agnon. I remember going to
bed that night, unable to fall asleep. I kept asking myself: how
can a son of mine grow up in a place where they worship Stalin?
The kibbutz was at the foot of Mount Gilboa, where our
ancestors had fought the Philistines and where King Saul had
fallen on his sword, the mountain cursed by King David. The
place is steeped in Judaism, in faith. An ancient synagogue was
discovered there; its mosaic floor is famous throughout the
world. I visited that synagogue with its remnants of the ark of
the covenant, its Jewish ornaments, the scroll of the sacrifice of
Isaac. You felt the divine presence there. Jews prayed there to
the God of Israel, and now my son worships a false god, the
cursed Stalin. I was angry at your blindness, your defective
education. I didn't know if I'd be better off getting rid of you.
I'll write about pious Jews, and my son will worship the Moloch of communism, heaven forbid!"

"That's how you felt?"

"Yes," my father replied. "I blamed your mother for sending
you to the kibbutz."

"I'm really shocked at your complaints about Mother. You
cut yourself off from us in 1935, and all those years you weren't
interested in my life, in what I did, except for a few emotional
letters you bothered to send."

"I wrote emotional letters?" asked my father. "My paternal

feelings were suppressed, almost dried up. I was never an emotional man."

I couldn't help laughing. "Maybe you wanted to smother your emotions, but you didn't succeed very well."

Later, I read him a letter he had written to me in 1943:

To my dear, beloved son!

Thank you very much for your letter. I'm so glad you're speaking, reading, and writing Hebrew. When I left for America, you were five years old. Now you're fourteen. I miss seeing you, talking and laughing with you very much. I have two pictures of you and when I look at them I miss you even more. As soon as the war is over, I'll try to come to Eretz-Israel, or you'll visit America. It's been a long time since I've written Hebrew. My beloved child, I love you very much. You're my only son and my soul is bound up with yours. I'm waiting for your letters. I want to know all the details. Do you like the kibbutz? Who are your friends? What do you read? How do you play in your free time? I don't want you to be sad for a moment. The victory over our enemies is approaching. It won't be long before I come to you or you come to me and then you'll tell me everything that has happened in your life from the time I left to this very day. Do you remember Polish or Russian or Turkish? What do you want to be when you grow up? Do you have talents for mathematics?

I kiss you with much love.

Your father,

Isaac

"That surprises me," my father stated. He asked to see the letter. I handed it to him, and he studied it a long time. His face grew soft and took on an embarrassed smile, as if he were caught in flagrante delicto.

"Yes, apparently I was once an emotional father. What effusion. If it weren't my handwriting, I wouldn't believe I had written it. Nevertheless, in those days, I didn't have a red cent."

"You never had a red cent, even when you brought me to New York."

Again, a heavy silence came between us. "You understand," he said after a moment, "I needed time. Your coming to New York caught me unprepared emotionally. I knew I was your father and I was loyal to you like every father is to his son. But I didn't know how to get to your heart. Your Yiddish was grossly inadequate. And so was your English. My old-fashioned Hebrew made you nervous. Your mother didn't bother to teach you Yiddish, of course. By the way, how is she?"

"Fine."

"You think I should see her?"

"What for?" I said, surprised.

"Curiosity," my father said. "You said she lives in Haifa, right?"

"Not far from here, in fact. But I happen to know that she's only recently managed to finally get you out of her heart and build a new life for herself. I don't think it's a good idea to open old wounds that have barely healed. You didn't even bother to tell her in 1940 that you had gotten remarried. She waited and waited, believing in your promises. Her memories of you have turned bitter. She hasn't forgotten, and she won't forgive. Is there any point going back to mutual recriminations?"

He conceded.

"Fine," I said. "Let's go over the translation of 'The Interview.' That's why you came, isn't it? Our conversation was also worth something," I remarked.

"Oh, of course."

We read the story together. I liked many of the corrections he suggested in Hebrew. As he read the translation, he deleted passages and even changed the content. My father maintained that brevity advances the plot, whereas a burden of descriptions renders it heavy. In *The Family Moskat,* in the Hebrew translation, the author leaves a glimmer of hope in the last chapter: groups of Zionist pioneers, at the beginning of the war, go off to Eretz-Israel singing "There in the Land of Our Fathers." And there the novel ends. In the English translation, that last chapter was omitted, and the book ends with the impending Holocaust: "Death is the Messiah. That's the real truth."

Haifa was gleaming. Lights flickered all over the mountain, the city, and the port. Blue lanterns glowed like jewels on the horizon atop the gigantic chimneys of the refineries in the bay. We stood on the balcony, admiring the sight.

"It is so beautiful and pure here. If only I could live here," he said to himself.

"Why don't you move to Israel?" I offered.

He chuckled at the suggestion, which had, he said, been made so often. Every Jewish activist or writer he met in Israel similarly urged him to move here. And now his own son was prodding him too.

"Late, too late. I've barely mastered English. To this day, I can't write about people who were born in America. Most of my heroes were born in Poland, even if they migrated to America. I'd have to live in Israel for years to describe it in my stories. In fact, where I live isn't important, because I never left Poland. Really, I still walk around the streets of Warsaw: Leszno, Marszalkowska, Krochmalna. Even if I write about a café on

Dizengoff, a refugee from Lublin will sit down at the table. Even in my previous incarnation, I was from Poland, in the time of the pogroms of 1648 and 1649, when Christianity and idolatry were all mixed up there. When I wrote *The Slave,* in my mind, I was in a remote Polish village, in the hut of the peasant Jan Bzik. A Polish sociologist visited me in New York and told me that *The Slave* is used at the University of Warsaw as an important source for the study of peasant religion and customs."

For a moment, my father closed his eyes and dredged up from the recesses of his mind a sentence from the Hebrew translation of that book: "In the distance, the sound of a mute yodel was heard, steeped in regrets."

"Gigi, do you happen to know what a 'yodel' is? I can't find it in the dictionary."

"The word 'yodel' is an onomotopoeia — taken from the sound of the ancient Swiss shepherd's horn that gathers the cows pasturing in the mountains. The singing imitates the curling notes of the horn."

Before we parted that evening, I wanted to know why in his letter to me he had inquired whether I had a talent for mathematics. He shrugged his shoulders, thought a bit, and said: "It was very hard in those days to make a living from literature. I hoped you'd grow up to be a scientist so you'd have an easier time of it than me. But the One who seems to determine human fate decided that we weren't chosen to be mathematicians."

12

DEMONS CAPER AMONG THE RUINS

In 1966, I returned to New York, this time with my family, for a second term as representative of my movement. In the course of those months, we visited my father several times, and it pleased me to observe that each visit seemed more natural and pleasant. My relationship with him became closer and actually took a turn for the better.

The day I came to see him, it was raining very hard. I found him sitting in his book-lined study, staring at the downpour. Turning to greet me, as if coming out of a trance, he shook his head and spoke at great length of the mystery and power of nature. He then got up and, from the shelves lined with his foreign editions, pulled out a Japanese edition of *Yentl*. He held it in his hands and, gently stroking the book, opened it and let his fingers lead him down the page. He pointed to one of the signs and said with a twinkle in his eyes: "There it is!" His finger stopped. "This one means *Yentl*, I feel it, I know it! I wonder how they pronounce *Yentl* in Japanese! How can my work connect with that culture? I can't imagine any of my books in a language I don't understand!"

Outside, the storm raged, lightning flashed, and thunder roared.

"The higher forces seem to be having a strong argument," he said, half to me, half to himself.

"About what?" I asked, amused.

Again, as he often did, he shrugged his shoulders. "There are many possibilities. Maybe a demon disguised himself as a rabbi and stole into a rabbi's wife's bed. And up there, in heaven, they're making a tumult about it."

It was dusk; the room was pleasantly dim. I pulled the Hebrew translation of *Satan in Goray* off the shelf and, at my father's request, began reading a few passages aloud. He wanted to hear how it sounded in modern Hebrew:

> In the year 1648, the wicked Ukrainian hetman, Bogdan Chmelnicki, and his followers besieged the city of Zamosc but could not take it, because it was strongly fortified; the rebelling *haidamak* peasants moved on to spread havoc in Tomaszòw, Bilgoray, Krasnik, Turbin, Frampol — and in Goray, too, the town that lay in the midst of the hills at the end of the world. They slaughtered on all sides, flayed men alive, murdered small children, violated women and afterward ripped open their bellies and sewed cats inside. Many fled to Lublin, many underwent baptism or were sold into slavery. Goray, which once had been known for its scholars and men of accomplishment, was completely abandoned.

"Are these authentic descriptions or made-up ones?" I asked my father.

He didn't answer right away, but after a few minutes he said: "These stories about the horrors of Chmelnicki and his Cossack murderers in every Jewish house in the shtetls in Poland are based on facts. As a child, I remember lying in bed at night, trembling with fear. I was scared of every barking dog, every whinnying horse, scared the Cossacks had come back to make a pogrom against the Jews. But I prepared a hiding place. I dug a pit behind the house and covered the opening with boards and scattered twigs over them as camouflage. The fear of Chmelnicki, cursed be he, hasn't left me since my childhood."

"You're talking about a childhood more than seventy years ago," I noted.

"I remember my childhood in Radzimin and my youth in Bilgoray very clearly to this day. In my head, I've restored my life from the age of two. I still remember the train trip from Radzimin to Warsaw when I was three years old. I rummaged around in my memory for a long time to recall the forgotten sights. First I remembered vaguely, then the picture slowly became clear."

"You can still describe Bilgoray?"

"Of course. Every house. Every street." For a moment he closed his eyes. The last rays of light came through the window. His face was pale, almost transparent. Now and then he blinked and frowned. His lips muttered. He remembered that the houses in Bilgoray were low, their roofs covered with tiles with moss growing on them. There was a marketplace in the center of the town, which was surrounded by Jewish houses and shops. A river flowed past the town, supplying power for two flour mills. "I can describe precisely the rooms of the house we lived in, the furniture, the bookshelf, and the place of every one of the holy books. If Jewish Bilgoray still existed, I would easily find my way around there." A Jewish atmosphere prevailed in that town, he continued, with its synagogues, Hasidic prayer houses, yeshivas, heders, a religious school for girls, and a ritual bath. His father, Rabbi Pinkhas

Mendel Singer, scion of a long-established rabbinical dynasty, served as the rabbi of Bilgoray.

"Incidentally," I told my father, "I recently heard a story about your father, which was written by Rabbi Yitzhak HaCohen Huberman, concerning a trial that is curiously reminiscent of King Solomon's judgment about the baby claimed by two mothers. Would you like to hear it?"

"Yes."

"It seems that the women of Krochmalna Street in Warsaw used to hang their laundry on the roofs. One woman stole a number of shirts from her neighbor, and the two women started quarreling about it. They appeared in your father's court, and after listening to the conflicting arguments, he asked them to bring him all the shirts they had laundered. They brought them, and after examining the shirts, he instructed your mother to add some of his own beautiful shirts to the pile. The next day, when the first woman came to hear his decision, he asked her to select which of the shirts in the bundle were hers. She chose hers. He then mixed the shirts up again and asked the second woman to identify hers. The second woman chose only the ones belonging to the first woman, as well as those of your father. That, of course, told the rabbi who the thief was. She admitted her guilt."

My father smiled and remarked: "I know the story. I may even have written about it, but not in the book *In My Father's Court.* So you, the grandson of such a glorious rabbi, have cut yourself off from the dynasty and joined Ha-Shomer Ha-Tsa'ir."

"I don't see you outfitted in Hasidic attire either," I replied.

"No, I'm not a rabbi, but I did study in a seminary for rabbis. You know, my grandmother, my father's mother, was a learned Jewess who wore a little tallis all her life and guided the women in the ways of Judaism. And my mother Bath Sheba followed her mother's example and studied the holy books and even the Talmud, and she could recite entire chapters of the Bible by heart. My father the Hasid was also a judge. In today's terms, he would be a psychologist and a sociologist and a lot of other kinds of 'ologists' too. He was a man who had a lot of feeling for the simple people: a fighter for social justice. He translated the *Choice of Pearls,* a collection of ethical epigrams, into Yiddish so poor people and women could read it.

"But didn't you ask me if the description in *Satan in Goray* is authentic?" my father asked me. "Yes, it is. The destruction and killing in 1648 and 1649 were so enormous that the atrocities of the Cossacks were passed down from father to son, just as the stories of the Holocaust now haunt us from generation to generation. In *Satan in Goray* I tried to describe the atmosphere of a pogrom, of the remnants of a slaughtered city, where demons caper among the ruins."

The room grew dark. For some reason, my father preferred not to turn on the light. He fell silent and watched the raindrops twisting down the windowpanes like snakes.

"Aren't the atrocities of the destruction enough? Why put demons among the ruins?" I asked.

"You're such a rationalist. Your father deals with demons and ghosts, and you still breathe the air of the Bolshevik revolution. What a contrast! I should write a story about the descendant of ten generations of rabbis who fell into the arms of Stalin and Lenin."

"I got away from them long ago. But you didn't answer my question."

He smiled. "You are still puzzled at my believing in demons and ghosts? Haven't I often told you that we're surrounded by invisible forces? Maybe in another thousand years we'll know more about them. For example, if we met a man in the street who lived two hundred years ago, he wouldn't know anything about electricity, or what electronics is, or how a telephone works. He wouldn't believe that you can send a manned missile into outer space, to the moon. It's silly to declare that we've reached the peak of progress. Schoolchildren in another twenty years will know things we have no notion of today. Why not accept that new entities will be discovered in the future? My son, such an 'entity' may even be watching us right now and laughing at us. Isn't that a wonderful subject for a story? It's hard to understand a person's behavior without the help of those entities. In my story 'Teybele and the Demon,' in terms of pure logic, Elhanan couldn't have gone into Teybele's bed and given her love and warmth. A love affair between Teybele and Elhanan wasn't possible in a shtetl. Only a demon who looked like poor Elhanan could bring joy and happiness to that wretched woman. Even though she knew that she was sinning, she throbbed with pleasure. Demons are part of our world. Only with their help can we understand what life is made of."

The phone rang. My father turned on the light and dashed to answer it. A lady from Long Island was on the other end. He kept repeating "Really?" "Indeed?" "You're sure?" and shaking his head. The woman caller had apparently lost the key to her apartment and had wandered around the streets in despair for hours. When evening came, she went to the subway station with the intention of going to her sister's house in Brooklyn. On the floor next to the ticket booth, she caught sight of a shiny metal object; she bent down, and lo and behold, it turned out to be the key to her apartment, she told my father. The woman was asking my father for an explanation. His answer to her was that one of the entities had "made sure" that she would find what she was looking for, protecting her from having to go to Brooklyn alone at night. Some time later, the story of the lost key appeared in at least two of my father's stories, in "The Key" and in "A Friend of Kafka."

While he was talking to her on the phone, I pulled a collection of his stories off the shelf and was leafing through them. I remarked to myself that many of his male protagonists are described as ugly men. Joel Yabloner, "The Cabalist of East Broadway," is described as "lean, his face sallow and wrinkled, [and he] had a shiny skull without a single hair, a sharp nose, sunken cheeks, a throat with a prominent Adam's apple." Morris Terkeltoyb of "Neighbors" is "short, broad-shouldered, with remnants of white hair that he combed into a bridge spanning his skull. He had watery eyes, a nose like a beak, and a mouth almost without lips." In "A Friend of Kafka," Jack Cohen "wore a monocle on his left eye, was stooped, [and] all that was left of his yellow hair was a meager fringe that bridged his bald head." Reb Mordecai Meir, of "Grandfather and Grandson," is "a small man with a yellowish-white beard, a broad forehead, bushy eyebrows beneath which peeped a pair of yellow eyes, like a chicken's. On the tip of his nose there grew a little beard. Wisps of hair stuck out of his ears and nostrils."

When I pointed this out to my father, he burst out laughing. His eyes twinkled, and he looked at me like a demon from his own stories. Pondering the matter for some time and ignoring my comments, he finally argued that being ugly didn't prevent any of his heroes from being happy, being praised, or lusting for women. There are outstanding skirt chasers among ugly men, and beautiful women are, in fact, often attracted to them. "There's beauty in ugliness, too," he added. "Ask women. Am I handsome? Sometimes I look in the mirror and I see my tormented face, my ears sticking out like a pair of fans, my sharp nose, my bald sloping head, and I don't understand what they

see in me. I love to describe miserable people. Ugly characters
are more interesting, made of materials that are also in me. I've
got a great love for schlemiels like Gimpel the fool. In fact, I'm a
schlemiel like that too."

His wife Alma reported that someone at her hairdresser's had
quoted a famous literary critic who had written that my father's
writing was nothing but sheer pornography. To prove it, the
critic had apparently compiled a list of descriptions of sex.
When Alma reported this to him, my father laughed: there's no
point arguing with literary critics, who are indefatigable seekers
of flaws in every literary work. "They're people who can't
create themselves, so they try to disgrace talented writers. To
praise a writer, all they need is a few sentences; but to tear him
to shreds provides wonderful material for a long essay."

"Isaac, you only appreciate writers who praise your works,"
interrupted Alma. "It takes only one word of criticism for you
to call such a critic a jerk."

My father waved off her words, but the subject was apparently still on his mind. "I've often been amused by my critics.
They always seem to know better than I what I meant in my
writing, and they also know why I failed. I write about love,
about lechery, about women who are unfaithful to their hus-
bands in some shtetl somewhere in Galicia. My critics argue
that I distort the character of the shtetl, as if they know it better
than I do. Was life in the shtetl sweet as honey? Wasn't there
lust? Yearning? Eroticism? I never write about the whole shtetl,
but about individuals. Pornography isn't literature, Alma, because it doesn't create the character of an individual, with his
lust and yearning. Pornography speaks in generalities, but you
won't find generalities in my stories."

We went out for a walk. The rain had stopped, and Broadway
was bustling again. Neon signs blinked on and off over the

The writer Isaac Bashevis Singer in 1987
in Miami Beach, where he spent the winter.
(PHOTOGRAPH BY RICHARD NAGLER.)

In Miami Beach, on the street named after him.
(PHOTOGRAPH BY RICHARD NAGLER.)

Isaac Bashevis Singer and his wife Alma.
(PHOTOGRAPH BY RICHARD NAGLER.)

Before the Nobel Prize acceptance ceremony,
the writer Isaac Bashevis Singer and his son. December 1978.

With King
Gustav XVI of
Sweden at the
Nobel Prize
ceremony.

Israel Singer (Zamir) as a child with
his mother Ronia (Rachel). Poland, 1935.

On a visit to Israel. Standing: the writer and his son. Sitting: his secretary
Dova Gruber and his grandchildren Merav and Noam.

The writer
and Alma
scattering
birdseed to
the pigeons.
New York,
79th Street,
1974.

The writer I. J. Singer, brother of Isaac Bashevis Singer,
his wife Genia, and son Yossl in the mid-1930s.

Isaac Bashevis Singer in his last year.

His last signature, when the disease was beginning.

Israel Zamir,
deputy editor of
Al Ha–Mishmar,
in 1974.

Israel Zamir–
the conquest of Eilat.
War of Independence, 1949.

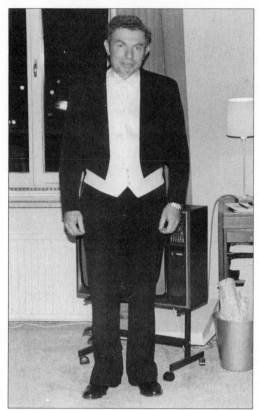

A kibbutznik in a tuxedo during the Nobel Prize ceremony, Stockholm. December 1978.

Israel Zamir's first passport. Residence: Haifa; Profession: Inseminator at Ha–On Institute in Sarid. 1955.

closed shops. A chilly wind blew from the Hudson in the west. My father pointed to the remains of buildings, where enormous cranes with long cables and big steel balls had pounded and demolished their walls, crushing them to bits. He told me that those apartments had been protected by rent control, and since the owners couldn't evict the tenants, they preferred to knock down the entire building and construct a new one in its place, thus multiplying the rent tenfold.

"My building will also be destroyed someday, and I'll have to look for a new apartment that will cost me a thousand dollars a month," he said sadly.

Broadway by night is different from Broadway by day. The neighborhood looked as if it had seen better days. The population of Harlem was slowly creeping southward, said my father, and as the blacks moved in, Jews were the first to leave the neighborhood. He was nostalgic about two kosher butchers and a delicatessen in the neighborhood, and he commented on the fact that violence was increasing, and it had become dangerous to walk around there alone. My father had actually been mugged recently by an enormous black man who had stopped him in the middle of the street, threatened him with a knife, and demanded his money. After my father gave him what he had, the hoodlum said, "Thanks, mister." And then the mugger disappeared.

"A polite mugger," my father commented ironically.

We continued our walk, and a big black dog dragging a leash came over to us, growling, and started sniffing my father's leg. We stood still. My father clutched my arm in panic; he seemed to be paralyzed with fear.

"He's going to bite me," he muttered.

I kicked the dog, who began barking loudly. His owner finally appeared and grabbed his leash.

"I'm sorry, mister. This dog usually only barks at blacks. You must be something special," he remarked with a loud laugh, and disappeared with his dog.

"He reminded me of Count Adam Pilecki, who used to set his dogs on the Jews," my father hissed in a trembling voice.

13

EXODUS '67

In May 1967, while I was still living in New York, the situation in the Middle East grew worse. The Straits of Tiran were closed by the Egyptians, the Israel Defense Forces went on alert, and the meetings held by Israeli Foreign Minister Abba Eban with the leaders of the major powers accomplished nothing. The nations of the world that claimed to support freedom of navigation weren't willing to do anything to open the straits and suggested that Israel appeal to the United Nations. An atmosphere of tension prevailed in the area, and letters from Israel hinted at preparations for an inevitable war.

My father sent for me. When I arrived at his home, I found him reading the newspaper. There was no television in his apartment, because he was afraid that it would disrupt his work. (Only in his last years, after Alma retired, did they buy a set.) The radio announcer reported that Nasser was solidly committed to the blockade and would respond to any Israeli aggression with an all-out war. My father was holding the afternoon paper, the *Daily News,* whose headline proclaimed: "The Mufti Calls for a 'Holy War'!"

"What will happen?" my father asked in a worried voice. "You think war will break out?"

"I'm afraid so. Moshe Dayan has been appointed defense minister, and all signs point to war." I told him about the phone calls we had received that day from Jewish organizations inquiring about the future of the summer youth programs.

"That's what interests them," he declared angrily, and shook his head.

I told him that the day before there had been heated debates at the Jewish Agency about whether to evacuate the youth movement students who had gone to Israel for a year's study. The local officials in New York urged that the students return to America along with all the other U.S. citizens, arguing that they couldn't be responsible to the parents for the fate of the young people in such an unstable security situation. One U.S. senator called and ordered us to bring his aide's daughter back from Israel, but the girl refused to return. As a Jew, she insisted that she had to participate in the war effort when her country was in danger. I asked the senator how he would respond if his country were in danger of war. The senator understood. But a few jittery Jewish Agency officials felt the need to apologize to the senator for "the arrogance of the Israeli representative."

That evening, I went to the 92nd Street Y with my father to hear a lecture by S. Y. Agnon, the Israeli Nobel laureate for literature. Dozens of admirers crowded around Agnon, and my father, who had wished to shake his fellow writer's hand, had to forgo that pleasure. "Too bad there aren't any translators so his books could be distributed widely," said my father. Later that night, some of the students in the movement and I went to Central Park. The impending war was on everyone's mind, and it was decided on the spot that all those who had finished their training would get passports and go to Israel at once to help. I was very impressed by those young American Jews, who were faced with life-and-death decisions for the first time in their existence.

"If we all go to Israel, what will happen to the summer camp?" someone asked. All of a sudden, summer camp seemed so irrelevant to us all.

When the meeting was over, I called my father to inform him that I might return to Israel with the students. He was scared and tried to dissuade me: "Gigi, don't go. I beg you." He hadn't called me "Gigi" in a long time.

Meanwhile, that Sunday, as scheduled, the Israeli Independence Day parade was held on Riverside Drive. I invited my father to come watch it with me. The weather was perfect. "God is on Israel's side," joked the newscaster. New York's police chief guarded the parade, which included brass bands and Scottish bagpipes. Riverside Drive was filled with people, young and old. The parade was led by Jewish activists. Republicans and Democrats wooing the Jewish vote were parading along as well. On the reviewing platform, the mayor of New York, John Lindsay, was seated, flanked by the writer S. Y. Agnon and the Israeli consul. Thousands of young people from Hebrew schools, Jewish community centers, and Zionist youth movements marched with the Israeli flag, demonstrating their identification with our beleaguered state. My father stood applauding with thousands of spectators on the sidewalk, watching in wonder as the Jewish sea flowed by. I suggested that he join the marchers, but he refused, reminding me that he didn't belong to any group.

After the parade, my father and I went out to lunch and watched the news on television in the restaurant. The film clips showed confident Israeli soldiers in the Negev, old men and yeshiva students quietly filling sandbags, and high school students calmly distributing mail in Jerusalem. Then the station shifted to its correspondent in Cairo, where a mob in the city square was shouting for revenge, waving their fists in hatred, and cursing Israel. An endless line of trucks loaded with soldiers, tanks, and armored carriers was driving through the streets of Cairo on the way to the Israeli border. In his mind's eye, my father saw an impending Holocaust; as for me, military cemeteries and bereaved parents were flashing through my mind.

"I'm glad you and your family are here," said my father.

"I'm trying to get back to Israel as hard as I can. Every few hours I call the consulate, but right now there aren't any planes," I told him. "I'll never be able to forgive myself for being away from my country in her time of need."

The following day, June 6, I called my father early in the morning to tell him that war had broken out. According to the radio, Egyptian forces were approaching Israeli borders by land and air. Mohammed El-Koni, the regular Egyptian delegate to the UN, had delivered to the Dane Hans Tabori, acting chairman of the Security Council, the Egyptian Declaration: "This morning, Israel deliberately began treacherous attacks against the United Arab Republic." He demanded that the Security Council meet immediately.

"A catastrophe is about to happen," said my father emotionally. "What does the American government say?"

"Robert McClosky, the State Department press secretary, claims that America will remain neutral 'in thought, word, and deed.' "

"That bad?!" A torrent of Yiddish curses landed on the head of that McClosky. "They can't allow another Holocaust!" my father shouted.

In this country, with its sensational news media, you can't remain indifferent. American radio quoted Egyptian and Jordanian sources who claimed that hundreds of tons of bombs had fallen on the cities of Israel and that thousands of dead and wounded were strewing the streets. Although we knew that the whole thing was exaggerated, we also knew that only a few bombs could cause terrible damage. I tried to get in touch with my mother in Haifa, but I couldn't get through to Israel by phone. I contacted the Israeli consulate in New York again, begging to return to Israel. "Instructions are to stay here. There are no planes. You can help from here. Don't believe the Arab countries' media. It's all a lie," they told me.

Is Israel defeated? Our students who had congregated at the offices of the movement were asking that question. All I could tell them was what I had heard from the consulate. They sat around the office helplessly, unable to do anything. Some of the girls wept, and others consoled them. The secretary of the movement finally took the initiative, distributed some blue "Keren Kayemet L'Israel" boxes, and urged everyone to go out and collect money. They were soon back, the boxes overflowing with coins and bills. The boxes were emptied, and the students went back out again. This went on repeatedly for a while. In the streets, groups gathered around our young people in blue shirts, eagerly pressing money on them.

That day, a leader of Hadassah burst into the movement office, begging us to help her organize the evacuation of Israeli children to a safe place such as Cyprus or Italy. "Let's at least save them," she shouted bitterly. We sent her away. We continued to sit and wait, frustrated by the lack of information. I called my father and told him about the contributions. He had heard that the United Jewish Appeal was accepting contributions and asked me to go with him to give money. The next day, on Seventh Avenue, I was overwhelmed to see a long line snaked around the UJA offices. Hundreds of Jews, some with tears in their eyes, waited patiently to make their contributions. The banner above the entrance enjoined them to "Give Till It Hurts."

"An exciting sight," said my father. "America preserves its neutrality, and the Jews give. Till it hurts." We joined the line. Ahead of us was an elderly woman who had come with her granddaughter, who had brought all her savings.

"This is my bas-mitzvah money; I'm giving it to Israel," she said.

"The world can't bear another Auschwitz," a rabbi surrounded by his students implored.

My father, tugging on my sleeve, whispered: "The world can bear anything."

That evening on television, an American general was reviewing the results of the war at the end of its first day. He seemed excited but gave restrained replies to the journalists' questions. In his opinion, the war was over. "Israel has done the impossible, destroying most of the Arab air forces in three hours. Three hundred seventy-four planes were set on fire and destroyed while they were still on the ground." The general went on to describe how the planes were attacked, what kinds of planes had been hit, and how the military airfields had been blown up. When he described the Israeli evasion of the radar systems, he lost his stiff bearing, and with admiration bordering on enthusiasm, he detailed Israel's splendid military achievement. As for the Arab armies' chances in the war, he continued with a brief smile flickering under his flat mustache: "In our day, can any power win a war without air support?" We were choked up. The telephone started ringing as excited friends called to congratulate us. When my father heard the news, he couldn't refrain from saying, "God finally came out of His indifference and decided to save His people."

We were called to the offices of the Jewish Agency, where thousands of students had crowded around the doors, demanding to go to Israel immediately. They all wanted to meet with

Israeli representatives. Each of us was asked to take a table on the ground floor and talk with them. I remember a young man from Queens sitting across from me with gleaming eyes; he could barely speak, he was so excited. Up to then, he said, he had ignored his Judaism completely, but when the war broke out, he suddenly felt that this was his fight. Judaism, he continued, had grabbed him by the scruff of his neck. His Jewish identity, suppressed up to then, had surfaced. Despite his obvious lack of battle experience, he was willing to do whatever had to be done, including dying for the state, he said, thumping his chest. One young person after another came and sat at my table, expressing the same sentiment. Every one of these American Jews, gripped by the recent Jewish trauma, had discovered his or her identity. They all wanted to join the people of Israel at once.

When I mentioned this to my father, he remarked: "It took a big, horrible war to make the Jews of America take stock of themselves. You have to do whatever you can to get them to Israel. Maybe this is the historical moment we mustn't miss. Don't pay attention to the government of Israel. Find ways to help them get there. You're saving a young generation of Jews who are facing assimilation." The government representatives explained to me, however, that they couldn't send young people to Israel because there wasn't anyone to take responsibility for them once they got there. Everybody was busy with the war effort. Not taking no for an answer, we contacted a Jewish ship owner who had once been in the Israeli navy. We explored the idea of sending a ship of Jewish youths to Israel against the instructions of the official institutions. The man, choked with emotion, immediately began calculating how many kids could fit on the ship he'd charter and how much food he'd have to order.

"In a week, the ship will be ready and waiting," he announced solemnly. "Meanwhile, you organize the students so they can board the ship at short notice; it will probably be anchored in New Jersey. And be sure to alert the journalists. We'll call it *Exodus '67.*' "

But the war ended too soon for the *Exodus '67* to sail for Israel.

Despite the initial victories in the war, some American Jews were worried. They knew what had happened to Jews in Europe in the past, and how America had kept quiet about it. Having learned their lesson, they were ready for action. The Presidents' Club, consisting of the presidents of the major Jewish organizations and the Jewish and Zionist establishment in America, was unable to accept the American embargo and organized a mass march on Washington to demand support for Israel. Although Israel had won victories, she needed a lot of help, starting with an airlift to fill the arsenals that had been depleted. There was no way to know when the war would end. I was on my way to Washington and invited my father to come along, but he refused: "They don't need me there," he said. "I'll pray for your success from here."

An enormous convoy of buses and cars made its way to Washington. We sang Israeli songs, and in our hearts, we were on the other side of the ocean, with our brothers and sisters. A big platform was erected on the Mall in Washington for members of Congress, liberal activists, folksingers, and Jewish leaders; with speeches and songs, they all condemned the treacherous policy of America. It looked as if most of the Jewish kids from Hebrew schools were there, along with their teachers and parents. Small children, who had been granted an unexpected holiday, ran around happily, buying ice cream, hot dogs, and soft drinks and waving Israeli flags.

As one of the members of Congress was speaking, one of the organizers of the rally, who seemed to have become its principal spokesman, interrupted him with an important news item. The crowd fell silent. In an emotional and trembling voice, the spokesman announced that the Old City of Jerusalem had been returned to the Israel Defense Forces. A bottle of wine popped up from somewhere, along with a silver goblet, and we heard the voice of a cantor intoning a blessing on the occasion. All at once the air seemed charged. I felt goose bumps. Roars of "Hurray!" burst from all sides. People spontaneously formed circles and danced the Hora. People were singing Israeli songs, clapping, and hugging one another.

I returned to New York exhausted by all the emotion. The next afternoon, I met my father in Steinberg's restaurant. He proudly introduced me to the owner, who offered me lunch on the house in honor of Israel's victories. People who heard that there was an Israeli in the restaurant hurried over to shake hands. And for a moment, I was a hero.

Broadway seemed changed to me. I could see many Jews proudly wearing buttons in their lapels with a Mirage jet on them and the phrase, "They did it!"

"Come on, son, let's go. We've got to feed the pigeons. This time we'll buy two bags of seeds. The pigeons also deserve a celebration."

14

FLOWER CHILDREN

One summer day in 1968, my father asked me to accompany him to a lecture he was giving at Queens College, sponsored by the Hillel Foundation. At the entrance to the campus, there was a slogan: "Slaughter Rats, Not People." My father was confused about what that meant. I reminded him of two current issues: Americans dying in the Vietnam War, and New York City cutting the budget for the war on rats in the ghettos. More injunctions and mottoes were in store for us as we made our way across campus: "Make Love Not War." "No, No, We Won't Go!" (i.e., to Vietnam). "Hey, Hey, LBJ, How Many Kids Did You Kill Today?"

There was worry on my father's face as we went to the cafeteria for coffee. "What do you think radical Jewish kids expect to hear from a writer like me?" he asked, his voice trembling with anxiety. All you had to do was glance at the kids in the cafeteria to guess that the lecture would be attended by a contingent of wild-haired hippies, the flower children of the New Left.

"Their Judaism doesn't mean anything to them; they reject it in their revolt against their parents. Don't be surprised if some of them show up wearing shirts that say 'Don't Trust Anybody over Thirty,' " I commented. He had never heard of that slogan. "America changes fast," I added. "This is no longer the America that admired Israel in the Six Day War. In the two years I've been away, Martin Luther King was murdered, and so was Bobby Kennedy. About a quarter of a million young people marched on the Pentagon, protesting the Vietnam War. There were riots in the black ghettos of New York, Detroit, Washington, Chicago, and Los Angeles. The campuses are in an uproar; police shoot students. There was a school strike in New York for seven weeks, and it was followed by an ugly wave of black anti-Semitism."

I explained to my father that the affluent American society had engendered a generation that was uninterested in the future; it wanted change now, immediately. That was the youth culture, which had no room for children, old people, or the family in general. They were concerned about the war in Vietnam and getting drafted. Then there was love, fun, drugs, psychedelic culture, and a frantic search for an independent identity. Most of them, I noted, were supported by their parents. I was aware that to be a radical revolutionary, you needed a good middle-class home. Although the New Leftist sometimes went hungry, he had a thousand-dollar stereo in his room. And he always knew that he had an alternative: all he had to do was call his parents, and the check would be in his hand. So they felt guilty because it was a phony rebellion. There were no proletarian youth among them, because those young people were working and didn't have time to demonstrate. Their characteristic leather jackets cost more than two hundred dollars; the Che Guevara boots cost a hundred and fifty. The absurdity of their lives made the youth pursue punishment. The ideal was to get arrested so that they could feel relief and continue on the revolutionary path. "Everything is rotten in the kingdom of

America. Everything has to be blown up and destroyed now!"
was their motto.

"What can I say to these kids?" asked my father. "Should I
talk about Judaism? Israel? Literature? I'm sure they haven't read
a single line of my work. Maybe I should cancel the lecture."

"That's up to you. But whatever you do, don't talk about
Israel. Unfortunately, the country is no longer an underdog. As
far as they're concerned, the worst thing that happened to Israel
was winning the Six Day War. The image of the Jew as Holocaust victim was wiped out and replaced by Ari Ben-Canaan,
the Sabra hero of Leon Uris's *Exodus*. They consider Jewish
schools, synagogues, community centers, and charitable agen-
cies as an evil establishment that collects money for Israel. And
if you're against the Establishment, you've got to be against
Israel."

"But you said that, during the Six Day War, a lot of Jewish
kids came to the Jewish Agency offices wanting to go to Israel
to fight and even die for the state," my father recalled.

"That's true," I replied. "But that was last year. After the war,
Israel sent heroes, senior army officers, who gave graphic descriptions of the conquest of the West Bank and the Gaza Strip.
And as for the kids here, the conquered Palestinians turned into
the Vietcong. They condemned Zionism for crimes against the
Arabs from the very beginning. They condemned them for
being allied with imperialism ever since Chaim Weizmann
appealed to the British government during World War I. And
they define the Sinai Campaign of 1956 as a complete coopera-
tion with Anglo-French imperialism; and now you've got im-
perialistic, militaristic, oppressive Israel driving Arabs out of
their villages, just like the Americans with all the slaughtered
Vietnamese villages."

"So what do I say to them?" My father was worried.

"If I were you, I'd read them a story."

"A story?" He became pensive, rummaged around in his briefcase for a while and pulled out a story, and his face lit up. "Yes, I'll read them 'Grandfather and Grandson,' about a Hasid who devotes his whole life to worshipping God and his revolutionary grandson Fulie who comes to hide in his house. The grandson is fighting the czar for a 'new world,' issuing slogans against the authorities, and arguing with his grandfather about the triumph of the revolution. The conversations between them remind me of the problems of the kids you just mentioned."

The Hillel representative joined us, and together we went to the lecture. Most of the audience were flower children with the typical wild hair, colored bands around their foreheads, fashionable leather coats, revolutionary boots, and kerchiefs tied around their necks; some were even barefoot. They had apparently come to enjoy themselves, not to listen. My father looked like their Establishment parents, and I was worried that they would laugh at him and taunt him. The guest lecturer was introduced, and a moment of silence followed. People were curious to know what this guy had to tell them. My father's face was tense, but he managed to smile at them. "I'm sure you'd rather see Rabbi Che Guevara here instead of me, but he's apparently hiding somewhere in the jungles of South America. So I'd like to read you a story you may find relevant. I'm worried that you'll soon discover, as Ecclesiastes says, that there's nothing new under the sun. You're not the first revolutionaries, and you won't be the last."

"Don't be so sure about that," spoke a voice from the back of the room.

My father ignored the comment and read his story from start to finish without interruption. From time to time there were mutters of identification with the revolutionary Fulie, who is finally murdered by the authorities. When he finished reading, they applauded. The question-and-answer period was next.

"You believe in God, right?" asked one of the students.

"More every day," replied my father.

"So maybe you know where your God was during the Holocaust. Why didn't He bother to save His followers from the ovens?"

My father answered that he did indeed believe in God, but that he too protested the Almighty's indifference to His people during the Holocaust, as well as all the crimes that occurred every day right in front of our eyes.

"You mean the Vietnam War?" someone asked.

"I protest against all bloodshed in the world. I'm a vegetarian, but not for religious reasons or for health reasons, but because I believe we have to take care of the cow and the chicken. Should a cow have to be slaughtered because we want to eat meat? What was her sin?" He surprised them.

"He's OK," the young man sitting next to me whispered to his neighbor.

"What about drugs? You think they should be permitted?"

I was afraid that my father would speak out against the drug culture and make them mad. To my surprise, he understood very well his audience and simply said: "Taking drugs is a private matter. Society doesn't have the right to tell an individual what to eat or what to sniff. Just as you can't forbid a stray dog to sniff rotten meat." They didn't seem to get the hint. Someone asked him what he thought of free love, and he looked as if he had been waiting for that one: "The famous philosopher Immanuel Kant defined the institution of marriage as a 'mutual agreement' to use the sex organ." Tempes-

tuous and prolonged cheering forced him to pause. Some of
the couples kissed passionately. Then he went on: "If it were up
to me, I would suggest that a man get married at the age of
seventeen, have children, and then get divorced twenty years
later and start the second part of his life. Then his children will
be grown up, on their own, and ready to start carrying out the
biblical injunction to 'increase and multiply.' " The audience
went crazy. Some stood up, whistled, waved their arms. They
clearly appreciated such answers coming from an aging Jewish
writer.

"Would you also allow legal abortions?" asked a pale girl.

"Of course. If a woman wants an abortion, who are we to
give her advice? Isn't she in control of her body?" This was also
greeted with enthusiastic applause.

A black student announced that his girlfriend was Jewish.
What did my father think about that? What did he think about
the oppression of blacks in the United States? My father lamented the serious crimes against blacks in the past. "We have
to do everything we can to make up for that crime," he said. He
had no objection to a black man marrying a Jewish woman; that
was strictly their business. As a Jew, he would be happy if the
black man would convert to our faith, because "we lost so many
millions of Jews in the Holocaust."

Then came the subject of Israel. A Jewish student asked my
father whether he thought it would have been better if Israel
had won fewer wars and allowed the Palestinians to win self-
determination and national pride. I was surprised by the question, which in my view could only have come from someone
who had never faced real danger in his life. I hoped that my
father would ask me to answer that question, but he seemed to
have forgotten my presence. He stressed the point that, as an
American citizen, he didn't think he had the right to advise

Israel, for good or for bad. In his opinion, every war is bloodshed and should be prevented.

Someone suggested that my father join the New Left philosopher-guru Professor Herbert Marcuse and collaborate on formulating the political platform. My father shrugged his shoulders in embarrassment; I don't think he had ever heard of Marcuse.

Finally, a girl stood up and wanted to know what Mr. Singer thought of the New Left protest movement. My father hesitated. I could see that he was wondering whether he could speak frankly. The spirit of confidence that had emerged between him and his audience also allowed for criticism: "I don't know enough about you," he said, "but my impression is that you're a movement without an appreciation of knowledge, even though you're students who have come here to acquire knowledge. Knowledge is a tool that helps you shape a worldview. But you've got everything backward: first you demonstrate, destroy universities, burn books, and then you formulate demands. You've turned the proverb 'Look before you leap' into 'Leap before you look.' You have no doctrine that includes the purposes of the movement. What will happen after you succeed in bringing down the governing establishment? Won't another establishment rise up in its place? And who will promise you that the new one will be better than the old?"

For a moment, my father returned to the story he had just read them:

> Reb Mordecai Meir clutched his beard and asked, "How do you know that a new czar would be better?"
>
> "If we have our way, there will be no new czar."
> "Who will rule?"

"The people."

"All the people can't sit in the ruling chair," Reb Mordecai Meir answered.

"Representatives will be chosen from the workers and peasants."

"When they get power, they may also become villains," Reb Mordecai Meir argued.

"Then they'll be made one head shorter."

The audience nodded, and someone spoke, admitting that they did need a revolutionary platform.

When the session was over, some of the girls came up to us and thanked my father; one of them even kissed his cheek.

"Madame, what is that pungent odor coming from you?" asked my father curiously.

"Ever hear of marijuana? If you come up to my pad, we can smoke as much as you want."

"And where do you live?" asked my father, who looked intrigued.

She wrote down her address on a slip of paper and gave it to him.

I had visions of coming to New York and finding them together at Steinberg's someday.

15

IN A HOTEL ON YOM KIPPUR

Shortly before Rosh Hashanah, during my father's visit to Israel in late September 1973, I invited him to the editorial offices of the paper *Al Ha-Mishmar,* where I work, to meet my colleagues. Most of them were from Poland, including his good friend Mordecai Halamish, his boyhood classmate from the prayer house at 19 Grzybowska Street in Warsaw. They seemed pleased to meet again. Halamish reminded him that in those years he had worn the Polish Hasidic attire of a long *kapote* or overcoat and a round black hat with a narrow brim, with his earlocks tucked up behind his ears. My father laughed, and they reminisced together for a while. He told some of the pranks of "Mordecai Flint," aka Mordecai Halamish. As usual, his reminiscences flowed over into personal memories of the Writers' Club at 13 Tlomacka.

One of the editors of my paper asked my father to explain his popularity among American Jews. My father repeated his hackneyed explanation — that American Jews used to see themselves as bastards, fatherless sons. The younger generation of Jews, the ones who were born in America, began asking questions: Who were their fathers? How did they live? How did they earn a living? Mendele mocher sforim's tales of the shtetl didn't offer them a satisfying explanation. Those Americans, the second-generation Jews, often told my father that it was thanks to his stories that they learned of their past and their parents' culture.

Someone at my paper pointed out that some of my father's work was controversial. They even accused him of "exploiting" the shtetl with his erotic and demonic writings. My father accepted the accusation and said that the late editor of *The Forward,* Abe Cahan, once asked him to stop writing about demons and ghosts and to focus on class exploitation in the sweatshops on the Lower East Side, where Jewish children and their parents worked sixteen hours a day. Cahan asked my father to inspect one of those sweatshops, maybe even try to work there for a few days, and write an article on the suffering of the tailors. "The paper should serve as a mirror for reality, not as an escape to heaven," Cahan told my father. Although someone should certainly write about the tailors, it could not be him, my father said. "I couldn't be original," he explained. Cahan, who admired my father and appreciated his talent, gave up the idea.

Another staff member of *Al Ha-Mishmar* criticized him for adapting his writing to non-Jewish readers, as if he were "winking" at them. Again, my father listened and didn't seem upset by the criticism. He told this man that the same charges had been leveled at Sholem Asch and Knut Hamsun. Hamsun's critics claimed that he had subjugated the Norwegian experience and language to the convenience of his European translators and readers. My father maintained that anyone who wrote for a translator or a foreign reader was doomed to failure. As far as my father was concerned, he was writing about universal subjects while really writing about Jews, rabbis, the sons of rabbis, yeshiva students, and holy implements — subjects he knew intimately, he had experienced. His writing, he said, was not merely about "Yiddishkeit" or Jewish life in general, but about Jews and Jewish life as it was, as he had seen it in Warsaw and Lublin. That was his historical-geographical circle: "I never did write and never will write about Bialystok, for instance. Of course there are difficulties in translation; but what artistic endeavor doesn't present difficulties of communication?

"Moreover," he continued, "the Gentiles don't want Jewish writers to write about them. Gentile writers should write about the Gentile experience, and Jewish writers about the Jewish experience. The more faithful their writing is to their people, the better the quality of the writing will be, and the better its distribution and resonance. I'd even go further and say that this is the reason for the limited success of Israeli writers who are translated into foreign languages. I know that a lot of them have been translated recently. But how many of their books are best-sellers? Why? Because most of them are Israeli writers and not Jewish writers."

After the visit at the paper, we returned to his hotel in a taxi with a Yiddish-speaking driver, which delighted my father; that apparently had never happened to him in America. He had met Hebrew-speaking cabdrivers in New York who were fresh from Israel, but no Yiddish speakers. "Yiddish is still alive in the streets of Tel Aviv," he said, looking me straight in the eye. "If a taxi driver speaks Yiddish with me, there's still hope." He stayed in the cab in front of the hotel talking for a long time. The driver told us how he had been saved from a death camp, and my father listened carefully. My father had a rare talent for making people speak. During his visit, I invited my father to come home with me to my kibbutz, but he had made appointments to see some friends from Warsaw and Bilgoray after Yom Kippur and declined.

Two days later, the Yom Kippur war broke out. I was soon

mobilized as a military writer and was sent to the Sinai. I tried calling my father at his hotel, but I couldn't get through. All the lines were tied up. I wasn't able to get back to Tel Aviv until three weeks later. I rushed to his hotel and asked the desk clerk if he was still there. He looked at me and said: "Are you his son? Go on up." He nodded. "He's been trying to reach you. And he's also been calling the airport all the time to find a way to get out of here."

I entered his room, and I found him sprawled on the bed, gazing up at the ceiling. When he saw me in uniform, dusty, with a rifle in my hand, he looked scared for a moment and gave me a terrified glance. Within seconds, he relaxed and smiled with relief. He jumped up and kissed me, glaring at my gun. Weapons were out of place in the room of a Yiddish writer, he told me, and he asked me to put it under the bed. "So you're still alive," he said with restrained joy, nodding at the ceiling as if to thank the Almighty. "Why didn't you call me?"

"I couldn't. Most of the time I was in the Sinai under fire, or traveling around. I saw terrible things."

"I know. I've been reading the papers. Are you hungry? Shall I order something for you?" he asked.

I glanced at him. His face was pale, almost transparent. There were dark circles under his eyes from lack of sleep; I could see that he hadn't slept a wink since the war had broken out. He didn't belong here and was trying to get a flight out of Israel. The Middle East conflict concerned him as a Jew, but not as an American citizen. He knew that there was nothing he could do to help. The city of Tel Aviv was blacked out; the streets were dark and empty. He refused to obey the sirens' command to go down to the shelter. If he was going to die, my father preferred to be in his room rather than in a stinking, crowded shelter. His Israeli friends were scattered; most of them had left town, some were engaged in the war effort. All his appointments were canceled. He felt stuck and couldn't write a word. "Every now and then an ambulance passes by, wailing," he said. "And I know that another family will be in mourning. I pray a lot. What else can I do? Yesterday at midnight, there were heart-breaking screams. I was scared and ran downstairs. The desk clerk said that an army team had come to the house across the street to announce that their son had fallen. They cried so much. I wanted to go and comfort them, but who am I? What would I say to them? I don't know Hebrew. Terrible, terrible. Every day I call the airport and they promise to get me out of here on the next flight."

Again, I invited my father to come home with me to the kibbutz, where at least he wouldn't feel alone, where he had family. Every evening, those members of the kibbutz who weren't mobilized would gather in the dining hall and watch television; they felt stronger when they were together. "You're living in an empty hotel, in a blacked-out city, it's no wonder you're depressed," I said. But again he adamantly refused my invitation. He didn't want to leave the city for fear of missing his outgoing flight. His bags were by the door, all packed. I showered and joined him in the hotel restaurant. The chefs had been called to the army, and the menu reflected this recent emergency. There were only a few items to choose from.

"Where are you coming from?" asked my father.

"The Sinai."

"The Sinai Desert? Moses wandered there for forty years. You didn't come on his traces, by any chance?" He was obviously trying to lighten the atmosphere with a joke.

"But I did meet a Moses there, a friend from my kibbutz. We were so happy to see each other. There I was in the middle of the desert, because our convoy was delayed. I was standing next to the car while some tanks were rumbling by on their way to the Canal. All of a sudden, one of the tanks screeched to a halt and the driver jumped out of the turret and started running toward me. I was completely surprised and froze for a moment, until I recognized my friend Moses. We hugged each other. I couldn't understand what he was doing there, since I knew that he was supposed to be on a tour in America. Because of the war he had returned to Israel. But not wanting his parents to worry, he hadn't told them that he was back.

"He had been touring the United States with a couple of friends, and the three of them were staying with a Jewish family in Washington State. Their hostess told them that she had heard something on the radio about 'some trouble' in the Middle East. It was from watching the television that they learned that war had broken out. 'As an officer in the armored corps with the highest rank of the three of us,' Moses said, 'I declared a state of emergency, and we rushed to the Seattle airport and left the car we had bought in the parking lot. It's probably still there. We got to New York as fast as we could. There was total chaos and an awful mess at Kennedy. An El Al plane loaded with essential equipment was about to take off. A communications officer told us that physicians and armored corps officers had priority for boarding the plane. All three of us were officers in the armored corps. When we landed at Lod, an army plane was already waiting for us and flew us directly to the Sinai. Since then we've been holding back the Egyptian advance. I haven't closed my eyes for forty hours.'

"He begged me not to tell his parents that he had come back, but I firmly refused. 'They've got to know the truth,' I said."

"The Israelis growing up in this country, the Sabras, are a

new Jewish phenomenon. In all of Jewish history, we have never known Jews to be eager for battle," my father commented pensively.

"When your country's in danger, you hurry home to defend it. It's not like in Poland when you did everything to avoid serving in Pilsudski's army," I said. "That wasn't your army, and Poland wasn't your own country in danger of being destroyed." We finished eating and went out. It was early evening. A wind blew from the sea; the street was deserted. The shop windows were dark and crisscrossed with tape. All of Tel Aviv's lights were ordered out. An army car dashed by. A civilian guard shouted at a house where a light could be seen flickering. In the street, which was usually lively and swarming with people, we were alone, trying to find a café open on Allenby Street, but every place was dark and closed. We continued walking.

"So you came here straight from the Sinai?" he asked, showing the same surprise and disbelief.

"Not exactly. I came from the Ministry of Defense."

"What were you doing there?"

"It's a sad story. This morning, I was in the Sinai heading north. I passed by an Arab village, and I saw a girl with a German shepherd standing in the middle of the desert, hitchhiking. One hand was holding the dog's leash and the other was clutching a sleeping bag. I picked her up. Her name was Irena Bugashvili; she was a new immigrant from the Soviet Republic of Georgia. Her husband had been mobilized on Yom Kippur, and since then she hadn't heard a word from him. Not a letter, not a phone call. After about ten days of silence, she took her dog and set out for the Sinai to look for him.

"There were many cases of soldiers who had gone to halt the enemy advance and had not been heard from. Irena combed all the bases and posts in the Sinai. No one had seen or remembered Simon. There seemed to be no trace of him. She met with senior officers, who tried to help her as much as they could and sent her from one unit to another. She was able to tell me all the names of the commanders and the bases by heart. Irena told me about a medical base she had visited where she had found a whole platoon on cots, shell-shocked. 'That was horrible,' she said. 'I went from bed to bed, looking at every one of them, looking but hoping not to find Simon. He wasn't there. If I don't search for Simon, it means I don't believe Simon's alive,' she said fervently. They had been married only a month before the war started. It occurred to me that Simon might have been captured by the Egyptians, and I suggested we go to the Department of Defense in Tel Aviv, where pictures of Egyptian and Syrian prisoners of war were shown. We sat there searching through pictures for a couple of hours. She didn't find any sign of Simon. Mothers and wives sat watching slides hoping to identify their loved ones. The weeping and moaning continued unabated. Several mothers clung to blurry pictures, claiming that they were of their sons; some women fainted. We left. Irena went to her sister in Bat Yam, and I came here."

Tears rose in my father's eyes. We returned to the hotel and hugged in a good-bye embrace. A call came from the airport, telling him that a plane was scheduled to take off for Rome in an hour. Grabbing his bags, he hurried in a taxi to the airport. I felt relieved to know that he would soon be safe, back with Alma in New York.

16

THE CITY OF TROLLS

At 2:30 on October 5, 1978, the Israel Army Radio announced that my father had won the Nobel Prize for literature. I wanted to remind him that, once again, he had been proved wrong. Back in 1966, we had been at his home in New York when we heard that Israeli writer Shmuel Yosef Agnon and poet Nelly Sachs had won Nobel Prizes for literature. My father seemed surprised and a little sad. He tried to restrain his emotions, but his hands trembled and revealed what he was feeling. For years he had been cited as a candidate for the prize. To a journalist who called him for his opinion on the Swedish Academy's decision, he replied that he was glad for Agnon and that one of Israel's outstanding writers had won the prize. He wasn't familiar with Nelly Sachs's poetry, he answered, but if the academy had granted her the prize, she must be good. Did he think that his chances of winning the prize were diminished? the journalist had asked. My father didn't even answer the question. He just shrugged, put down the receiver, and gazed at the telephone for a long time. He remained depressed for the rest of the day.

"So, dear father, you may have to give up the dream of the Nobel Prize," I remember saying to him then.

He grimaced but said that the greatest writers in the world — Tolstoy, Dostoyevsky, Gogol, Knut Hamsun, and many others — hadn't won it either. Real writers don't write for prizes, he declared. Writing is a longing, a lust; without that, a writer can't do anything.

"But a Nobel laureate's books are widely distributed. Don't you want yours to be read all over the world?" I asked.

He turned to me and suddenly burst into a strange laugh. "Listen, I had the weirdest dream last night. I found myself in a house with a room made of straw." His eyes closed, and his forehead furrowed to dredge up details from the dream.

"Maybe it was the village where Jacob the Slave was?" I suggested.

"Could be. At any rate, I was in the house of one of the peasants."

"Jan Bzik?"

He laughed: "If you want, let it be Jan Bzik."

"Was Wanda there too, by any chance?" I asked cheerfully.

He twisted his mouth and blinked, but that beautiful woman apparently hadn't been conjured up. He remembered sitting at a rough-hewn table. The peasant thrust a knife into a loaf of fresh-baked bread and gave my father half of it. Then, lifting a pot of boiling water, he pulled a chicken out. Ripping a drumstick off, he gave it to my father and then poured brandy out of a leather bag. "We guzzled like beasts of prey," he recalled. "When the meal was finished, the peasant wiped his mouth on his sleeve. I got up from the table, walked around the room, and went to a wooden bookcase. There, next to statues of demons and amulets, was a book of mine, its binding filthy with grease spots. It was *Satan in Goray*. I was so glad. I asked the peasant if he had read the book. Removing the bottle from his mouth for a short moment, he winked at me as if to say yes. I laughed until I woke up. Yes, to answer your question, it is very important to me to have my books distributed all over the world," he said. "But even if I thought no one would ever read them, I'd still go on writing."

In 1976, his friend Saul Bellow, who had translated *Gimpel the Fool* into English, won the Nobel Prize for literature. Upon hearing the news, my father sighed and told me that he wished his friend success. At the time he seemed resigned to never being one of the winners himself. His own chances for the desired prize were nil or, as he put it, "a withered noble Nobel blossom."

Today, as I was listening to the announcement over the radio, I felt pride and an immense joy. My colleagues at work brought out a bottle of wine and toasted in my honor. It was strange to be receiving congratulations for something I had had absolutely nothing to do with. Partaking in an unearned success seemed wrong, somehow.

Almost immediately, journalists rushed to my house, participating in their own way, I guess, in the celebration. I had barely walked in the door of my home that evening when a large number of reporters were asking me to search through my family albums for pictures of my father. Our twenty-year separation and reunion were brought up again. Questions of all kinds were coming at me at the same time. Was my father surprised about the Nobel Prize? My father had given up on winning the prize, I told them. Because the Nobel had already been awarded to so many Jews in recent years, he had thought that there was no longer any possibility of him winning. As his son I was overjoyed, and as a writer I believed that he certainly deserved it.

Telegrams were pouring in. The president of Israel, Yitzhak Navon, along with some Knesset members and many of my fellow journalists, rushed to my apartment to congratulate me. As expected, my father's phone was busy all day. It wasn't until midnight that I was finally able to get through to my father in the United States. Could I travel to Stockholm with him, both as his son and as a correspondent of the Israeli newspaper *Al Ha-Mishmar*? I asked him. He agreed, and, feeling exceptionally expansive, even offered to send me a plane ticket.

Unable to contain myself, I asked him a journalist's question: "Where were you when you learned about the prize, and how did you react?"

"You too?! I was having breakfast at Sheldon's restaurant in Miami when a phone call came for Alma. She was excited and said that one of her friends had heard on the radio that I had been given the Nobel Prize for literature. 'It's probably a mistake,' I told her, and went on eating. But she persisted. 'If it's true, we better finish breakfast first,' I said."

I congratulated him and hung up.

A month and a half later, as I went through passport control at Kennedy Airport in New York, a black immigration official glanced at my documents and asked me the usual question: "Do you have relatives in America?"

"My father," I replied dryly.

"Mister Zamir? Where does he live?"

"His name is Isaac Bashevis Singer, and he lives in Manhattan, on 86th Street and Broadway."

"You mean the guy who won the Nobel Prize?" she asked curiously and grinned.

"Yes."

"I read *Enemies, a Love Story*. Interesting book." She gave me an amused glance, and suddenly her eyes lit up: "So you're the son of the Polish woman, Yadwiga?"

That night she'd have a tale to tell her friends. I told the incident to my father. "I'd rather have one reader in Harlem," he said, "than a hundred scholars at Columbia University."

My father's apartment was transformed into a communications center; his living room was now a multimedia studio. It looked as if a television crew had made themselves at home there. Cameras flashed, journalists were asking questions, radio broadcasters shoved microphones in his face. My father seemed to fare extremely well on this new stage. He was having a fine time with it all, sitting comfortably in his armchair. Alma tried to make her way past the tripods, cameras, and journalists. She was attempting to reach him to tell him that I had arrived, but the photographers wouldn't let her through and pushed her away. She was, they complained, blocking his face from their view. I stood among the pack of journalists for quite a while before he noticed me. My father was definitely enjoying being a star, I thought. He had spent most of his life being an anonymous writer, the brother of the well-known I. J. Singer. Now his moment had arrived; it was his turn to enjoy the limelight. His face was beaming; he was cracking jokes; the bons mots were flying. He suddenly noticed me in the crowd, stood up, came over to where I stood, and kissed me. He introduced me as his son and made a point of telling the reporters that I had come especially from Israel; he asked the television crew to include me in their broadcast. But clearly, this was not my day. They weren't at all interested in me, and, exhibiting the usual courtesy of journalists the world over, they asked me to clear out of their way so they could concentrate on the Nobel laureate.

That afternoon, a television crew freshly arrived from Poland came to his home. Even the country he had left so long ago considered it a national honor that the winner of the Nobel Prize — like the Pope — had been born there. My father was still fluent in Polish; he had, after all, spoken that language for the first thirty-one years of his life. But when the interviewer asked him questions in Polish, to my surprise, he said that he preferred to answer in English.

"I haven't spoken Polish in forty-three years. I understand the language, and you can ask your questions in Polish, but on Krochmalna Street in Warsaw, we spoke Yiddish, not Polish," he told the interviewer, who seemed disappointed at first.

Could he remember exactly where he had lived in Warsaw? they asked my father, and the interviewer pulled a map of prewar Warsaw out of his briefcase. My father's eyes lit up; he snatched the map out of the man's hands and, tracing the way with his finger, made his fingers walk around the streets of Warsaw. He found his Krochmalna Street; then Leszno Street, where we had lived until we all left Poland. From there, his square finger strolled to Marszalkowska Street; the Vienna Station; the Bristol Hotel, where in those days, all the well-to-do merchants stayed; Gnoina Street, the Jewish commercial center; and the building of the Writers' Club at 13 Tlomacka Street. Did the streets still exist? he asked them. But the members of the crew didn't know.

"In that building of the Writers' Club, I met Peretz Markish, H. D. Nomberg, and Kaganovski for the first time. I remember the wall over the stage where the portrait of I. L. Peretz hung. It was a temple of Yiddish literature," he recalled excitedly.

They were clearly embarrassed; being of a younger Polish generation, they had never heard of any of those famous characters. He continued to rattle off the names of cafés in the area and, again, asked the interviewer if these still existed. As before, the interviewer shrugged and admitted that he didn't know.

"The Nazis have destroyed everything," sighed my father. He didn't take his eyes off the map. He muttered the names of the streets and was as excited as a boy. I could see how his beloved city once more rose up before his eyes. He found and named the street one of his mistresses had lived on and told us how he used to bribe the doorman of her house to let him in. The Polish television crew filmed an excited writer returning to the landscapes of his youth. When they were finished filming, my father asked to keep the map as a souvenir.

Unlike my previous New York trips, when I would routinely visit my father after his morning writing, I didn't get to see much of him in those days. He spent his mornings preparing for the events of the Nobel ceremony and devoted his afternoons to giving interviews to the media. He was so besieged by the media that he finally had to leave home and rent a hotel room, where he and his secretary Dvora Menashe worked over the course of several days on his various speeches for the Swedish events — both the ones he was expected to give and other speeches for unforeseen occasions. My father was faced with a serious dilemma: should he deliver his speech in Yiddish or in English? It was a serious decision. If he spoke in Yiddish, he knew that most of the audience wouldn't understand him. He pondered for days. At the end, his need to present the Yiddish language to the world prevailed. Isaac Bashevis Singer would give his Nobel acceptance speech in the language that had ultimately won him world renown.

"Who knows if Yiddish will ever be heard again in the palaces of Stockholm?" he said. On the other hand, one could argue that he had lived in the United States for forty-three years. He had written all of his works in Yiddish there, and it was through their translation into English that he had acquired millions of readers. Didn't English also deserve to share some of the honor? After endless debate and anxiety that went on for days, my father found what appeared to all of us to be the right compromise: he would deliver the first part of his speech in Yiddish and the rest in English.

Off to Stockholm he went. Leaving from New York, my father was accompanied to the Nobel ceremonies by a group of close friends that included Roger Straus and Robert Giroux, of Farrar, Straus and Giroux, the American publisher of all his books; Roger Straus's wife, Dorothea; Shimon Weber, the editor of *The Forward;* Rabbi Berkowitz; the author Paul Kresh; and two of Alma's friends from Miami Beach.

As for me, I flew on a different flight to Stockholm and landed on December 7, at three in the afternoon. The city was already dark. In Israel, by contrast, at the same hour in the afternoon, you have to keep your sunglasses on. For me, Sweden seemed exotic and bizarre, of course. It was cold and windy. It was early afternoon, and night had already fallen. During the summer, I was told, the day died at midnight. I immediately sensed an incomprehensible depression. A kind of pervasive melancholy came over me in those dark and gloomy streets. Low clouds had gathered over the city, and the street lamps were barely visible in the fog. I had expected to arrive in a shining city where Nobel Prize winners poured in from all over the world; instead, I found cold, fog, and darkness. I was disappointed.

One of the display windows attracted my attention. It was crisscrossed with strips of black, blue, and red plastic supporting hundreds of trolls — the little Scandinavian demons with evil, cruel faces. I had read somewhere that, according to an old Swedish legend, at twilight they emerged from their lairs and tempted humans to sin. Those demons are known for their evil, and woe to anyone who falls into their hands. I stared at the window display for a few minutes. The atmosphere had the eerie quality of an Ingmar Bergman film.

My father had always talked and written extensively about his demons. But his demons, I told myself, are jolly. They tell a happy tale, create a sharp joke. He had made me feel that they were closer to human beings. It occurred to me then, as I was looking at this window filled with the little Swedish demons, that this city of trolls was uncannily appropriate for my father, whose stories of demons had been written in a dying language.

I reached the hotel, where my father and his entourage had already settled in. The magnificence of the royal suite that had been given to my father, with its sparkling crystal chandeliers, was dazzling. I was overwhelmed. Every few minutes, a different group of dignitaries in their gala attire came in, offering formal congratulations to the Nobel laureate. My father shook hands warmly, bowed, kissed the ladies' hands, and generally behaved in a manner that to me looked artificial. I felt ill at ease. I didn't recognize the father I knew. He seemed to have donned the mantle of success in a way that bothered me. I kept this to myself. I was worried that this new flow of praise and splendor would make him forget the worn-out shoes of the heroes of his stories — the paupers of the shtetl. He was acting like a movie star, superficial, strewing what looked to me to be phony smiles like a Hollywood celebrity. This change in his behavior annoyed me; I had never seen him like that. Later, when we were alone for a moment, I told him what was bothering me.

His forehead wrinkled, and his face grew dark. His blue eyes bored into me. My father didn't brook criticism, and he looked angry. Was this the time to settle old accounts? If he wanted to tell me to go to hell, he refrained. But it was clear to me that I had offended him. We sat silent and withdrawn, like a pair of snails. It was five in the afternoon and black as night outdoors; the wind was wailing. I had hoped that the praise and glory wouldn't dazzle him, but apparently they had. Glancing at his face, I felt a storm brewing there. I was sorry that I had spoiled the celebration.

He finally got up and walked over to me. He put his hand on my shoulder, looked at me softly, and in the tone of a worried father, said: "Don't worry, son. Celebrations pass like a night-blooming flower that opens for a moment and then closes. Money and honor were never my main concerns. For a moment only I am visiting the temples of Stockholm, I am shaking the hands of kings and nobles; but in my heart the pauper still exists. I'm aware of the danger lurking at my door. When the ceremonies are over, I'll go back home to that bathrobe I've been wearing for the last forty years, to the same house slippers. I won't let the adoration get a foothold in my life. What does a writer like me need? Fine furniture? Expensive art? I'll go on getting up at seven every morning, sitting in the same chair, and writing my stories on my knee. Don't worry, son, I'll go on being the same Isaac Bashevis Singer you've known, the same horse that needs a whip to turn the manuscript in to the editor on time. No, I'm no movie star. With all the glory and adoration, I'd be far happier if I could go to my father's prayer house on Krochmalna. After all, who am I? An aging Jewish author, who writes about demons and ghosts."

17

TRYING ON A TUXEDO

According to tradition, the Swedish Royal Academy provides every Nobel Prize winner with a Volvo, a driver, and a liaison person from the Foreign Ministry during his visit in Stockholm. My father's liaison was Ruth Jacoby, whose task was to ensure that my father got to all the planned events on time and to stave off any pests who might plague him. One of the latter was a local industrialist, a Jewish activist who insisted on inviting my father to dinner at his home, where he had invited dozens of Yiddish speakers, the crème de la crème of Jewish society. My father didn't feel that he could refuse, but Ruth Jacoby intervened, suggesting that the man leave my father alone because his schedule was packed. The industrialist was not a man to give up; he had been preparing the banquet ever since hearing that Singer had won the Nobel Prize. He was an important activist who organized readings of Yiddish literature and subsidized the publication of Yiddish books. Didn't he deserve a bit of reward and some pleasure too? Ruth Jacoby stood firm. He decided to lie in wait. He would catch my father when she wasn't around.

That evening, my father and his guests were invited to a cocktail party given for all the winners. My father put himself in

Ruth Jacoby's hands and obeyed all her instructions, including what to wear to each event.

We arrived at the auditorium, where we were to meet the other laureates. The photographers were already waiting; we were blinded by their flashbulbs. They were running from one Nobel Prize winner to another, positioning them in various poses and asking them to shake hands and smile happily. My father was still smiling with genuine pleasure. He was celebrating a double victory: that of a successful writer who had made it to the top, and that of a representative of a godforsaken language that had now achieved world recognition. He constantly reminded me of that and never concealed his pride. I can still see my father posing and shaking hands with Professor Peter Leonidovich Kapitza, a prominent Soviet physicist of Jewish origin. As a young man, Professor Kapitza had left the Soviet Union and moved to Great Britain; but in 1934, he visited Russia and didn't return to Britain. Kapitza's wife, son, daughter-in-law, and a few stern-looking young men were also in the photograph. Later, Ruth Jacoby whispered in my ear that these men were KGB agents assigned to make sure that the distinguished scientist didn't defect to the West and give away state secrets. Keeping a close watch on him, they followed him wherever he went, like his shadow. His son told me that, back in Stalin's time, his father had refused to pay proper homage to the dictator. Subsequently, he had been removed from his scientific post for several years. Only after Stalin's death was Kapitza able to return to the physics institute. Professor Kapitza was short, wore glasses, and didn't have much hair. At eighty-four, he was the oldest of the prize winners and walked with a cane. For years he had headed the Soviet Institute of Physics in Moscow. My father tried to exchange a few words with him, but the physicist's son regretfully told him that his father didn't speak

English. Ruth Jacoby's eyebrows shot up; she remembered that the famous physicist had published his basic work in English and that she had even heard him lecture in that language. He had received strict orders "from above" not to speak English, we found out later, because the KGB agents didn't know the language very well and would have had trouble following conversations. The photographers finished their photo session, and the professor parted from my father, smiling. He clasped his hands upward, as if to say: "That's how the regime is, and there's nothing to be done."

Professor Daniel Nathans, short, balding, and bespectacled, hurried toward us, his face beaming with joy. He had won the prize for his research in microbiology. Director of a research institute at Johns Hopkins University in Baltimore, Professor Nathans told us that he had recently spent a semester at the Weizmann Institute in Rehovot; he lavished enthusiastic praise on the institute, its staff, and Israel in general. His wife taught Hebrew at a Jewish high school in Baltimore, and while they were in Israel, she had worked as a volunteer on a kibbutz. They had read all my father's books and were thrilled to meet him. Although my father had received compliments before, he nonetheless always blushed. The soft light in the hall helped conceal his excitement.

"Professor Nathans, do you really work with an electronic microscope where you can see molecules, atoms, and electrons?" my father asked in wonder, his eyes wide with curiosity.

The microbiologist smiled and waved dismissively: "That's nothing compared to you, a distinguished artist who can write such marvelous stories. Your work is infinitely harder than mine." And so they stood, complimenting each other and clutching their champagne glasses.

The party ended close to midnight, and we all retired to our respective suites. Suffering from jet lag, I woke up at four in the morning, picked up one of my father's new books, *A Young Man in Search of Love,* which I had bought before boarding my flight, and discovered biographical details about him I hadn't known before. In his youth, my father had a girlfriend who was twenty years older than he, and she taught him "selected chapters in the lore of life." He often recommended that young men have relationships with older women. Up to then, I had thought that it was just a view he espoused. In reading *A Young Man in Search of Love,* I discovered that he had lived through it all personally. He described how he had been on his way to a whorehouse in Warsaw but had recoiled at the last minute and had run away. I found that description in *A Friend of Kafka,* but there it's Kafka who flees, not my father.

At ten o'clock the next morning, we met with eighteen members of the Royal Swedish Academy of Literature. These distinguished members devote their time to reading books and conducting extensive discussions to select the Nobel Prize winners, until the white smoke rises from the chimney in early October. My father and I were impressed by the academy building, which looks like a palace; every door is carved, every piece of furniture is a work of art. The members of the Swedish Academy wanted to hear my father's opinion of their writers, and he obliged, giving a creditable performance and hoping to convey the impression that he was an expert on their works. Although he wasn't familiar with a great many Swedish writers, he gave great praise to Knut Hamsun, Strindberg, Ibsen, and other famous Scandinavian writers whose books he did know well. Then a discussion of the eloquence of Yiddish literature followed, his home field, and he mentioned his brother I. J. Singer, Shalom Aleichem, and Mendele mocher sforim.

Some of the members of the academy asked my father

whether *The Forward* still appeared. In the 1930s, my father told them, the paper had sold about a quarter of a million copies. Today, the circulation had dwindled to thirty or forty thousand. At *The Forward,* "they tell the story of a Yiddish newspaper editor who looked out the window, saw a funeral, and told his assistant to print one less copy." (A few years later, the paper shifted from a daily to a weekly.)

That afternoon, my father and I were taken by Ruth Jacoby to a special store, where we were to rent our formal attire. Shimon Weber, the editor of *The Forward,* tried his suit on first; my father grinned at him. "You look like a real schlemiel," he couldn't help saying. But a few minutes later, when it was my father's turn to put on trousers that were too wide and too long on him, Shimon Weber returned the compliment: "You walk like Charlie Chaplin. You'll be a big hit!"

The young tailor had a hard time fitting my father. He was taking special pains to ensure that the space between the jacket and the trousers was no bigger than five centimeters, and nothing seemed to please him. The formal trousers were too baggy, and the tailor explained to Alma that they were to be held up by suspenders. My father looked in the mirror; he was unhappy. The coat didn't fit properly across his back. The poor tailor was at a loss. He pulled out another suit, and Alma continued to make a face; then came a third, which she also rejected out of hand.

"The demons don't want a Jewish writer to appear in a tuxedo, but in a *kapote,*" said my father. The tailor brought out another suit; he hadn't heard of Isaac Bashevis Singer, but he remarked that, for him, the "Nobel week" was "one big head-ache."

As we were trying on our respective tuxedos, the persistent industrialist–Jewish activist appeared out of nowhere with a sonorous "Shalom aleichem," announcing that after our fitting session, we were invited to attend a banquet at his house. My father stared at him with an amused expression and inquired: "May I ask how you earn your living?"

"I manufacture stockings."

"Stockings? And it's a big business?"

"Quite big."

"So you must be a real lunatic. Why do you neglect your business and devote your time to Yiddish? I really have to write a story about you."

We resumed our fitting with the tailor.

My father was unable to decide whether to go to the banquet or not, and Alma carried on her argument with the young tailor.

"Mr. Singer, can you explain why half the Nobel Prize winners seem to be Jewish?" asked an Israeli journalist who had followed my father to the tailor.

My father became pensive. An amused expression came over his face. Breaking into a smile, he said: "The Holy-One-Blessed-Be-He apparently invested Himself body and soul in the Jewish people. It's a crazy people. A marvelous people. A very strange people."

"And other peoples, how did He create them?" the journalist persisted.

"Other peoples are just peoples," he said. He didn't elucidate what he meant by "just," but those who knew him understood what it meant. Once after visiting the Western Wall in Jerusalem, my father was asked by a journalist what he thought of it. "Just another wall," he answered.

18

TO FIND A YIDDISH TYPEWRITER

The hall of the Swedish Academy was packed with people, all dressed in their gala clothes. In the center, on a platform, was a table with a bouquet of flowers and a glass of water. On three sides of the platform, chairs were lined up for the eighteen members of the Academy of Literature, ruddy Nordic intellectuals, the literary elite of Sweden, who had selected my father to be the Nobel laureate and had come to listen to his talk. What did these Vikings have to do with Jewish literature? I wondered. Could they understand the misery of the shtetl? Could they fathom the existence of a deprived and persecuted minority? I knew, of course, that they had probably read most of my father's books, and some of them had even said that it was the mystical aspect of his writings that had won their hearts. Apparently, according to many people we spoke to in Stockholm, there was a distinct affinity between the Jewish demon and the Scandinavian troll. In the back of the hall, I could see the Israeli ambassador Mordecai Kidron, his entourage, and the leaders of the local Jewish community, for whom today's ceremony was a very special celebration. After all, it wasn't every year that a Jew expressing himself in Yiddish won the prize. My father informed the members of the academy that he would open his speech in Yiddish. "No one ever spoke Yiddish in this ancient and honorable hall," he stated. The eyebrows of Dr. Gyllensten, the secretary of the academy, shot up in mute surprise, and the ceremony began.

The next day, with a twinkle in his eye, my father remarked that a Jew in New York might be surprised to find a few lines of Yiddish on the first page of the *New York Times.*

As my father entered the hall, waving his newly tailored tails, he was greeted with a long standing ovation. Before reading his prepared remarks, he explained to the audience of Swedish scholars that Yiddish was "a composite of medieval German, Hebrew, and words borrowed from other languages." Then he began his Yiddish address:

> The high honor bestowed on me by the Swedish Academy is also a recognition of the Yiddish language — a language of exile, without a land, without frontiers, not supported by any government, a language which possesses no words for weapons, ammunition, military exercises, war tactics; a language that was despised by both Gentiles and emancipated Jews. The truth is that what the great religions preached, the Yiddish-speaking people of the ghettos practiced day in and day out. They were the people of the Book in the truest sense of the word. They knew of no greater joy than the study of man and human relations, which they called Torah, Talmud, Musar, Kabbalah. The ghetto was not only a place of refuge for a persecuted minority but a great experiment in peace, in self-discipline, and in humanism. As such, a residue still exists and refuses to give up in spite of all the brutality that surrounds it.

The Swedes listened politely to what must surely have seemed a totally incomprehensible language. He then switched to English. On Friday, the headline in *The Forward* read: "Bashevis Singer Opened His Nobel Speech in Stockholm in Yiddish."

> The storyteller and poet of our time, as in any other time, must be an entertainer of the spirit in the full sense of the word, not just a preacher of social or political ideals. There is no paradise for bored readers and no excuse for tedious literature that does not intrigue the reader, uplift his spirit, give him the joy and the escape that true art always grants. Nevertheless, it is also true that the serious writer of our time must be deeply concerned about the problems of his generation. He cannot but see that the power of religion, especially belief in revelation, is weaker today than it was in any other epoch in human history. More and more children grow up without faith in God, without belief in reward and punishment, in the immortality of the soul, and even in the validity of ethics. The genuine writer cannot ignore the fact that the family is losing its spiritual foundation. All the dismal prophecies of Oswald Spengler have become realities since the Second World War. No technological achievements can mitigate the disappointment of modern man, his loneliness, his feeling of inferiority, and his fear of war, revolution and terror. Not only has our generation lost faith in Providence, but also in man himself, in his institutions, and often in those who are nearest to him.

He paused a moment and raised his tormented face to his listeners before he settled the historical account of a persecuted people:

> In their despair a number of those who no longer have confidence in the leadership of our society look up to the writer, the master of words. They hope against hope that the man of talent and sensitivity can perhaps rescue civilization. Maybe there is a spark of the prophet in the artist after all.
>
> As the son of a people who received the worst blows that human madness can inflict, I have many times resigned myself to never finding a true way out. But a new hope always emerges, telling me that it is not yet too late for all of us to take stock and make a decision. I was brought up to believe in free will. Although I came to doubt all revelation, I can never accept the idea that the universe is a physical or chemical accident, a result of blind evolution. Even though I learned to recognize the lies, the clichés, and the idolatries of the human mind, I still cling to some truths which I think all of us must accept someday. There must be a way for man to attain all possible pleasures, all the powers and knowledge that nature can grant him, and still serve God — a God who speaks in deeds, not in words, and whose vocabulary is the universe.
>
> I am not ashamed to admit that I belong to those who fantasize that literature is capable of bringing new horizons and new perspectives — philosophical, religious, aesthetical, and even social. In the

history of old Jewish literature there was never any
basic difference between the poet and the prophet.
Our ancient poetry often became law and a way of
life.

Some of my cronies in the cafeteria near the *Jewish
Daily Forward* in New York call me a pessimist and a
decadent, but there is always a background of faith
behind resignation. I found comfort in such pessi-
mists and decadents as Baudelaire, Verlaine, Edgar
Allan Poe, and Strindberg. My interest in psychic
research made me find solace in such mystics as your
Swedenborg and in our own Rabbi Nachman
Bratzlaver, as well as in a great poet of my time, my
friend Aaron Zeitlin, who died a few years ago and
left a spiritual inheritance of high quality, most of it
in Yiddish.

The pessimism of the creative person is not deca-
dence, but a mighty passion for the redemption of
man. While the poet entertains he continues to
search for eternal truths, for the essence of being. In
his own fashion he tries to solve the riddle of time
and change, to find an answer to suffering, to reveal
love in the very abyss of cruelty and injustice. Strange
as these words may sound, I often play with the idea
that when all the social theories collapse and wars and
revolutions leave humanity in utter gloom, the
poet — whom Plato banned from his Republic —
may rise up to save us all.

There was total silence in the hall. My father then proceeded
to read in English a passage he had previously delivered in
Yiddish:

My father's home on Krochmalna Street in Warsaw
was a study house, a court of justice, a house of
prayer, of storytelling, as well as a place for weddings
and Hasidic banquets. As a child I had heard from my
older brother and master, I. J. Singer, who later wrote
The Brothers Ashkenazi, all the arguments that the
rationalists from Spinoza to Max Nordau brought
out against religion. I have heard from my father and
my mother all the answers that faith in God could
offer to those who doubt and search for the truth. In
our home and in many other homes the eternal
questions were more actual than the latest news in
the Yiddish newspaper. In spite of all the disenchant-
ments and all my skepticism, I believe that the nations can learn much from those Jews, their way of
thinking, their way of bringing up children, their
finding happiness where others see nothing but misery and humiliation.

   To me the Yiddish language and the conduct of
those who spoke it are identical. One can find in the
Yiddish tongue and in the Yiddish style expressions
of pious joy, lust for life, longing for the Messiah,
patience, and deep appreciation of human individu-
ality. There is a quiet humor in Yiddish and a grati-
tude for every day of life, every crumb of success,
each encounter of love. The Yiddish mentality is not
haughty. It does not take victory for granted. It does
not demand and command but it muddles through,
sneaks by, smuggles itself amid the powers of destruction, knowing somewhere that God's plan for Creation is still at the very beginning.

   There are some who call Yiddish a dead language,

but so was Hebrew called for two thousand years. It has been revived in our time in a most remarkable, almost miraculous way. Aramaic was certainly a dead language for centuries, but then it brought to light the Zohar, a work of mysticism of sublime value. It is a fact that the classics of Yiddish literature are also the classics of the modern Hebrew literature. Yiddish has not yet said its last word. It contains treasures that have not been revealed to the eyes of the world. It was the tongue of martyrs and saints, of dreamers and Kabbalists — rich in humor and in memories that mankind may never forget. In a figurative way, Yiddish is the wise and humble language of us all, the idiom of frightened and hopeful humanity.

The talk lasted twenty minutes, and the applause went on for another five. As usual after his speeches, my father called for questions, ignoring Dr. Gyllensten, who was sitting next to him. Someone opened the discussion by asking why none of his books had ever been published in Yiddish.

"My books did appear in Yiddish," he replied, "but they sold out, and there were no second editions. When a Yiddish publisher succeeds in selling an edition of two thousand copies, he knows a miracle has happened and he thanks God. Miracles don't happen every day, so he doesn't risk his slim profits on bringing out another edition. With the prize money, I hope to get my works published in Yiddish."

A pious Jew remarked that my father wrote about the Hasids in Poland but not about Hasids in America, and he asked if my father thought that the two traditions were close. "Of course there's a great similarity," he answered, "but there's also a big difference. We know that youthful experiences are deeper than the impressions we get in old age. That's why I write about Hasidism in Poland. Back in Poland, a Hasid was a Hasid twenty-four hours a day; but in America he's a Hasid and a merchant and a lawyer and a businessman. He hasn't got time to be a Hasid twenty-four hours a day. Nevertheless, Hasidism is preserved in its own way. Human beings die, but not cultures. Not even Hitler and Stalin could kill Jewish culture."

The chief rabbi of Sweden wanted to know if there was a difference between the spirit of Hebrew and the spirit of Yiddish. "There are two kinds of Hebrew," explained my father. "Ancient Hebrew — of the holy books — and modern Hebrew. I first went to Israel in the 1950s and wanted to know how you hail a cab in Hebrew. A friend of mine replied: 'A lucky thing you asked today, because just yesterday the Hebrew word for taxi was born.' Yiddish has no ancient and no modern, and that's the main difference: Yiddish has the spirit of days gone by, but you can't enumerate the components of the atomic bomb in it. Hebrew is brand-new. Some people say that Yiddish is a sick language, but wise men know that the difference between a sick language and a dead language, as Yiddish was once defined, is like the difference between a sick man and a dead man."

"Mr. Singer, your books have been translated into fifty languages. Will you get to a hundred and fifty next year? And another question: You said in an interview on Swedish television that you're looking for a Yiddish typewriter. Did you find one?"

"My books have only been translated into sixteen languages. That's what I said to an interviewer, but there was a mistake in the article he wrote, and the number sixty appeared. To this day I've been trying to consign that error to oblivion. Maybe now I'll get to sixty languages. In my day, I've seen a lot of lies that turned into truth, and vice versa. As for the type-writer, for years now they haven't manufactured Yiddish type-writers, only Hebrew ones. I'm afraid that even my prize money won't be enough to buy two new Yiddish typewriters. Maybe I'll make an appeal on television for a Yiddish type-writer. I've got an old typewriter, forty-three years old, which has turned into a literary critic for my many sins. Whenever I write something it doesn't like, it breaks down. I send it to the typewriter repairman, but it ignores him and considers only literary values."

The audience cheered that answer. Someone whispered in my ear that such loud laughter hadn't been heard in that hall in years. The Jewish entertainer made them laugh uproariously. My father charmed them with his modesty and his rich Jewish humor.

Then a Swedish scholar with a perfect Nordic face stood up and asked my father's opinion of Professor Martin Buber, who had rewritten the books of Reb Nakhman of Bratslav.

"Reb Nakhman of Bratslav was one of the great storytellers in the world and a marvelous man. Professor Martin Buber discovered him and rewrote his stories. He shouldn't have done that, because the stories of Reb Nakhman of Bratslav should be left as they are. Once I got a copy of a book titled *The Complete Works of Shakespeare Expanded and Improved* by somebody named Horowitz." This line was greeted with thunderous laughter and applause, and when it died down, my father went on: "I don't intend, God forbid, to compare Professor Martin Buber with Horowitz. All I mean is that the best version of the stories of Reb Nakhman of Bratslav is his own."

At this point, Dr. Gyllensten, anxious to stick to the time-table, thanked the laureate in the name of the academy. For a little while, the previously cold hall of the Swedish Academy had been turned into an almost warm yeshiva.

19

THE OWNER OF A HEAD OF CABBAGE

It was Saturday morning. There was an uninterrupted drizzle over Stockholm. From the window, all I could see was a thick fog. A howling wind whirled the leaves around. The main synagogue of Stockholm had sent a car for us. It was a Reform synagogue, because a more traditional one would have forbidden driving on the Sabbath. At the entrance to the synagogue, a battery of photographers wearing black skullcaps stood waiting. As the car arrived, the hum of television cameras began and didn't stop until we left.

The local rabbi greeted my father in Hebrew, shook his hand warmly, and ushered us all inside, where we were welcomed with the tones of an organ. The cantor and the rabbi wore long black robes with stiff collars, and for a moment I thought I was in a church. Then a loud applause came from the balcony, where women were waving handkerchiefs. I was surprised to see the women sitting separately, as in an Orthodox congregation. Above the women's section, the choir sang an Israeli song. Two big white candles were lit on both sides of the ark of the covenant. The prayer began in Swedish and then in Hebrew.

Professor Daniel Nathans, Dr. Arno Penzias, and my father were invited to take the seats of honor at the eastern wall, next to the ark of the covenant. At the entrance, people had been handed skullcaps, prayer shawls, and prayer books. The cantor trilled the prayer, and a man next to me, assuming that it was his duty to keep me informed as to the progress of the service, occasionally leafed through my prayer book, pointing to the spot where they were reading. The cantor had a beautiful voice and was accompanied by the organ and choir.

"About a hundred years ago," the man sitting next to me explained, "a Jewish congregation came here from Germany. They were profoundly influenced by 'reform,' and the result was this 'hybrid,' women sitting apart from men." The prayers sounded more like Italian opera than Hasidic melodies.

My father glanced occasionally at me. He looked deep in prayer, and I could see his lips moving incessantly. He also seemed to be absorbed in the bilingual prayer book. He no doubt must have been thinking how different things had been in the Hasidic prayer house on Krochmalna Street. From time to time, I watched him bury his face in his hands. I wondered if he was asking God to give him strength to get through all the ceremonies and receptions he was facing today.

Each of the Nobel laureates was invited up to the Torah, and each in his own way intoned the blessing, and the congregation responded. My father recited it in the clear Ashkenazi accent he was used to. That day's bar mitzvah boy read his assigned scriptural passage, and the rabbi carried on with a sermon on the biblical passage of the week, drawing a parallel between Jacob's dream and the dream of a more enlightened humanity. He concluded the service by blessing the Nobel Prize winners and their guests.

Ruth Jacoby urged us on: we were expected at the American embassy. On behalf of the prize winners, Dr. Penzias, a refugee who had fled to the United States with his family before Hitler came to power and was now a famous physicist, blessed the congregation. When services ended, many worshippers crowded around the Nobel winners, hoping to shake their hands. But a nimble group of ushers led them straight out to the cars, and we soon arrived at the American embassy.

We stood in a long receiving line. I introduced myself as Isaac Bashevis Singer's son; that, of course, triggered the inevitable questions of why my father's name was Singer and mine Zamir. Unwilling to explain ad infinitum, and to simplify things, I decided to name myself Israel Singer for that day. Waiters were passing drinks, and the tables around us were heaped high with delicacies. We were then invited to lunch, with the sound of American country music being played in the background. My father and the ambassador sat next to each other and seemed absorbed in conversation. Again, I could see how much he was enjoying himself. The next event, later that afternoon, was a reception by the Nobel Prize Fund in the library of the Academy of Literature. The same Swedish Royal Academy members we had met the day before were present at the library.

It was a very happy day, and I was surprised at how well my father seemed to endure all the festivities.

On Saturday night, we were guests of the Jewish community of Stockholm. When we arrived, a standing ovation awaited us. A young woman greeted us in Yiddish, and someone sang. It was festive and moving. A woman read a story from *In My Father's Court*. The cameras were constantly snapping. My father felt extremely comfortable in this Jewish atmosphere, where many people spoke Yiddish with him. He was smiling and joking and was asked to deliver a few remarks. Climbing onto the stage, he pulled out of his pocket a piece of paper.

Some time ago, a helpless translator came to me and asked: "Mr. Singer, please tell me, how do you translate into English: *Er iz a veykher mentsh, a diamant?* In every language in the world, a diamond is the hardest material, but in Yiddish it's soft. Should you translate it as 'a man soft as a Jewish diamond'?"

English, they say, is the richest language in the world. The last edition of *Webster's Dictionary* contains almost three-fourths of a million words. But I argue that Yiddish is much richer, maybe not in technical words, but undoubtedly in estimating human nature and qualities.

I'll prove it. How many words does English have for "poor"? Maybe half a dozen at the most. But in Yiddish we've got pauper, beggar, destitute, wretched, shlepper, good-for-nothing, owner of a cabbage head, shirtless, miserable pauper, deep in grief, chopped grief, and just everyday grief. You can say that a man swallows his saliva, that he forgot the shape of a coin, that he drops dead from hunger three times a day, that things go as bad for him as for a wicked person in the next world or a saint in this world, that he carries his soul on the end of his nose. You can say that he stumbles like a fool, that he barely has enough for water and grits, that all year long is Passover for him, since he doesn't see a slice of bread. You can even call him Rothschild, with a slight wink, and everyone will understand that he's dying of hunger. Only a crazy person would trade such a rich language for English.

The audience burst out laughing. Every expression was greeted with applause. My father was asked to go slowly so they could absorb all the words. As the laughter finally died down, he continued:

> By the way, how do you say "crazy" in English? Crazy, childish, and if you want to be more technical, you say schizophrenic or paranoid and all the other expressions that don't have a Jewish flavor. The Americans themselves, when they want to express madness with a Jewish flavor, say: "He's meshugga." But in Yiddish, a man can be mad, crazy, turned around, mindless, confused; he can go out of his mind, have a screw loose, or a valve, have no head, not know what world he's living in, not know what mother gave birth to him. He can jump the tracks, be a savage in human form, lose his noodleboard, and so on. True, I do admit that in terms of automobiles and airplanes, Yiddish does have problems. But is it so bad if a Yiddishist takes the bus or subway?

The Jewish audience went wild with laughter, and the Swedish journalists, who didn't understand Yiddish, felt left out.

Dr. Penzias, the other Nobel laureate, who had been asked to say a few words, had to wait quite a while until the audience calmed down.

"When I was told that I had received the Nobel Prize," Dr. Penzias began, "I was flooded with phone calls and was invited to a reception at my synagogue in Chicago. I ran to my tailor. He's a 'hardboiled' guy. I rushed to him and told him that I had to be fitted for a tuxedo that night because I had to go to a UJA reception. The guy's face fell, he pulled his thick eyebrows together, and said: 'Tonight? No way.' I went on begging and pleading, explaining that I had to appear on television and that it was terribly important. But the tailor wasn't moved by my plight. Finally, in my despair, I decided to let him in on the secret: 'I don't know if you read the papers today, but you know that . . . that . . . that I won the Nobel Prize.' The tailor's mouth opened widely; then he smiled, raised his eyebrows, and said: 'What?! You're Isaac Bashevis Singer?' "

20

WALKING WITH A PRINCESS

It snowed all night. The streets of Stockholm were all white, and the cars parked at the sides of the roads looked like sleeping white bears. The royal ceremony was to be held in the afternoon. Ruth Jacoby dutifully reviewed all the details of the ceremony with my father. If "her" laureate made a mistake, God forbid, her position at the Foreign Office could suffer. The Nobel ceremony is a grand and noble affair for everyone, and the Swedes take the ceremony extremely seriously. My father wasn't used to a set script. He was best when he could be spontaneous and generally preferred to ad lib. There was no room here for improvisation or last-minute flashes — and that made him very nervous. He reread his speech over and over, and at eleven o'clock, he was picked up and taken to the concert hall for a dress rehearsal.

Paul Kresh, one of my father's biographers, had come to Stockholm with us. I invited him to go for a walk. Drawing the hotel lobby curtain to the side and peeking at the gloomy sky and dancing snowflakes, he showed no enthusiasm for the invitation to tromp around. He forcefully suggested that we stay in the warm lobby. My son loved horses, I told him, and I had promised to bring him a riding hat from Stockholm. Rather reluctantly, he decided to join me. It was a sleepy Sunday afternoon. We passed a few women in the street on their way to church.

We found most of the stores shut, with the exception of one hat store, where we found nothing so outlandish as a riding hat on a snowy day. We finally found what I was looking for in a small sport shop, and thoroughly frozen, we made it to a café.

The Swedes set a quota of guests for each prize winner and were very strict about it. Alma had invited her two friends from Miami Beach to all the events, and Paul Kresh, despite being my father's close friend and biographer, often found himself outside the hall. He pleaded with me to ask my father to include him in all the Nobel events.

"How can I write your father's life story if I don't attend all the events?" he lamented.

I informed my father of Paul's request the next day, and he replied that he didn't need biographers. The events of his life were the events of his books and stories. "Change the name of the hero of the story and you've got a record of my licentious life. So why do I need biographers?"

At three o'clock that Sunday, my father returned from the dress rehearsal, and Ruth Jacoby gave him high marks for obedience and good behavior. The main ceremony was to begin in an hour and a half. We struggled into our tuxedos with her assistance. She then gave me an envelope with a round white button inside. "That button admits you to the Throne Room, where His Majesty will receive you right after the ceremony." One final inspection. Ruth Jacoby adjusted the handkerchief in my father's coat pocket and straightened my bow tie.

The limousine hurried us to the ceremony in the municipal concert hall. A bevy of photographers was massed in the doorway, blocking the entrance. We had a lot of trouble getting in. A few professors of the academy were already sitting on the stage. Many wore medals on their chests, and it reminded me of World War II Soviet generals. War medals? I asked myself: when had Sweden been in a war lately? I later learned that people in Sweden receive awards for civilian public service.

A full orchestra was tuning up in the gallery. On the floor right above it, the television cameras were being positioned. Brightly lit by an imposing chandelier, the stage was divided in two: to the left were the four chairs destined for the royal family, to the right were nine chairs reserved for the Nobel Prize recipients. A Swedish flag was hanging over the stage, and beneath it was a banner with the number 1978 embroidered on it. The chandelier was also casting a strong light on the red velvet chairs. As the hall began filling up, I admired the women dressed in the latest fashion and the men all in tuxedos. Most of the people seemed elderly to me. Every year, I was told, this ceremony was repeated with perfect precision, just as Alfred Nobel had stipulated in his will. The audience always included the Swedish nobility, senior government officials, directors of the Nobel Fund, ambassadors whose citizens had won the prize, famous publishers, and diplomats.

At precisely four thirty, a horn was blown and the audience fell silent. The king and queen appeared on the stage in royal splendor, and everyone stood up. Behind the royal couple, the prize winners filed in with slow, measured step. I recognized my father's fair head. He was marching somewhat pensively, as if the whole thing had nothing to do with him. The chairman, a member of the board of the Nobel Fund, Professor Son Bergstrom, welcomed the prize winners and read a speech on the developments and achievements of science.

The king and queen sat with great dignity across the stage

from the nine prize winners. The king looked a bit bored. During the speeches, I caught him fidgeting and peeking at his watch. The award ceremony was long: it began in the concert hall of Stockholm, continued in city hall, in the inside courtyard, in the weavers' guildhall, and ended in the Blue Room on the second floor. It lasted over two hours. My father had been warned that the dinner would take another three hours.

One by one, each of the professors delivered a speech on behalf of the Nobel Prize Fund about the scientific achievements of "his" prize winner. Then the person was awarded a medal and a document from His Majesty. My father was introduced by Professor Lars Gyllensten, secretary of the Swedish Academy. Describing his achievements, Professor Gyllensten concluded: "Many of his characters step with unquestioned authority into the pantheon of literature where the eternal companions and mythical figures live, tragic and grotesque, comic and touching, weird and wonderful — people of dream and torment, baseness and grandeur." He emphasized my father's contribution to art, whose roots were in the Polish Jewish tradition, granting to literature universal values. My father stood up straight and strode to the king. He said later that as he walked he felt as if he were bearing the great mass of Yiddish-speaking Jews, then added after a moment: "If only my brother Joshua Singer were here with me."

The trumpets blared. The king and queen stood up, followed by the line of Nobel laureates, and in a splendid procession, they all began making their way to city hall, each with a lady of the royal court on his arm. Professor Kapitza took the queen's arm, and my father walked with Princess Christina, the king's sister, who was considered the smartest member of the royal family. He joked all the way with her, and I could see that she was trying with all her might not to burst out laughing. Later, when

I asked him what he had said to Christina that was so funny, he gave me an amused look and replied: "Mind your own business." After the banquet, four of the Nobel Prize winners were asked to deliver thirty-minute speeches. My father was the first:

> I am often asked why I write in a dying language. I like to write about ghosts and a dying language is most suited for writing about demons and ghosts. The deader the language, the more alive the ghost. Ghosts like the Yiddish language, and as far as I know, they all speak it. I believe not only in demons and ghosts, but also in resurrection. I'm sure that someday, millions of Yiddish-speaking corpses will rise out of their graves and that their first question will be: "What's the latest Yiddish book?"

Everyone was smiling. Swedes are accustomed to frozen, restrained, dry speeches, and here was a Jewish troll, melting the ice. He went on:

> There are five hundred reasons why I began to write for children, but to save time I will mention only ten of them.
>
> Number 1. Children read books, not reviews. They don't give a hoot about the critics.
>
> Number 2. Children don't read to find their identity.
>
> Number 3. They don't read to free themselves of guilt, to quench their thirst for rebellion, or to get rid of alienation.

Number 4. They have no use for psychology.

Number 5. They detest sociology.

Number 6. They don't try to understand Kafka or *Finnegan's Wake.*

Number 7. They still believe in God, the family, angels, devils, witches, goblins, logic, clarity, punctuation, and other such obsolete stuff.

Number 8. They love interesting stories, not commentary, guides, or footnotes.

Number 9. When a book is boring, they yawn openly, without any shame or fear of authority.

Number 10. They don't expect their beloved writer to redeem humanity. Young as they are, they know that it is not in his power. Only the adults have such childish illusions.

The time had come for everyone to gather in the ballroom, while those who had "white buttons" — family members of the winners — were invited to the Throne Room for a meeting with the king and queen. We stood in line, with an official in royal livery reminding us to bow deeply to His Highness. My father glanced at the royal couple and whispered in my ear: "Would you believe it? It's even nicer than the movies."

The king looked tired as he shook hands indifferently and smiled politely. Next to him stood a prompter who gave him details and informed him about the families and suggested questions.

Our turn came. My father bowed, I followed suit, and then there was an awkward silence. What on earth do you say to a king? I wondered. Our tongues seemed paralyzed, and even the king looked a trifle embarrassed. What does a Swedish king have to say to a Yiddish writer? My father was the first to collect himself, and said: "Your Highness, I am very glad to be here."

The king: "Yes, well, of course."

My father: "It's hard to believe all the wonderful things I've seen here."

The king: "Yes, of course."

The prompter whispered something to the king and pointed at me. His Majesty nodded and said: "I hear that you and your son haven't seen each other for twenty years. Well, that's very interesting."

My father: "Oh, yes, that was some time ago."

The king: "I'm told that the two of you wrote a story about that encounter."

I: "There was a book with two stories describing that encounter."

My father: "I'll never again let my son answer my stories with his own."

The king: "Well, yes, of course." Silence.

Finally, my father said: "I'm very happy with your reception for a Yiddish writer."

The king: "Well, yes, of course."

Silence. Then the prompter hinted that this "exciting" audience was over, and another family approached to take their turn.

We went into the room reserved for important guests and were offered glasses of champagne. My father looked tired and decided to forgo the rest of the festivities. We returned to his hotel as the Swedes undid their collar buttons, stuffed their bow ties in their pockets, and danced uproariously to strains of the Beatles.

21

SCORN OF YIDDISH

My father's life was no longer the same after his return from Stockholm. He couldn't feed the pigeons on Broadway anymore because passersby always recognized him from the pictures in the papers and on television. They would tell him how proud they were of him or how much they enjoyed his books. He would smile with embarrassment and thank every one of them personally, and he seemed genuinely glad. He was sincerely happy to emerge from his longtime anonymity. The praise intoxicated him. He walked around the streets of New York like a bridegroom on his wedding day, with everyone praising and congratulating him.

Despite the spontaneous celebrations that seemed to erupt each day for him, my father insisted on reassuring us that the prize hadn't gone to his head. He still kept a proper sense of proportion and claimed that he wasn't impressed by those external symbols of success. I was touched to hear my father talk modestly to Natan Shaham, the Israeli cultural attaché in New York. Natan Shaham went so far as to say that Sweden had received my father too sympathetically. They understood his books, Shaham said. His books were simple and clear, and he knew that anybody could get something out of them. Like all northern peoples, the Swedes were just a little bit anti-Semitic and seemed glad to find thieves, adulterers, liars, pimps, and simple dirty characters among the Jews in his books.

In autumn 1979, I returned to New York and immediately went to visit my father. Passing by the store on our way to lunch, my father stopped to buy birdseed. The owner was glad to see him, refused to take any money for the sack of seeds, and requested an autograph for his grandchildren. But the times when my father was able to feed the pigeons in peace were over. He scattered seeds to the wind, but the pigeons wouldn't come down from their roofs because of the crowd that had gathered around him. He raised his head sorrowfully at the recalcitrant pigeons and continued walking. Men and women constantly stopped us in the street, asking my father for his autograph. Journalists and photographers appeared out of nowhere and clung to him. He resented these invasions.

The telephone in his apartment seemed never to stop ringing. Everybody he knew from way back considered themselves part of the celebration and invited him to their homes. For these callers, the idea of having dinner with a Nobel laureate was irresistible. My father spent his time refusing, apologizing, and confronting constant solicitors. He could no longer write and asked the telephone company for an unlisted number. Up to then, he had been proud that anybody could call and talk with him. No more. His walks along Broadway had become more of a burden than a pleasure. Most of the time, he found a trail of onlookers in his wake. Sometimes he looked out his window to discover photographers and television crews lying in wait across the street. He gave up his daily walks. Freedom was over. Like a movie star, he was no longer a private citizen, and that upset him.

One day when I arrived at his home I found him striding

around the strip of grass in the inner courtyard of the apartment building. He had become like a prisoner getting his daily exercise. I joined him. Walking around and around in such a small space was exhausting and boring without the bustle of the street. A few onlookers stood at the gate of the building, peeping at the miserable writer walking in circles. The doorman had been instructed not to let them in. That was the price of fame.

One weekend, I suggested to my father that we go out of town to escape his admirers and the media. I thought it would be interesting to visit Liberty, New York, the resort town where the Ha-Shomer Ha-Tsa'ir movement summer camp was. He wasn't particularly wild about the idea, but since he hadn't been out of his house in a few days, he finally agreed.

We found the summer camp, which was empty because it was autumn. The students had departed at the end of the summer, leaving behind a mess of blankets, torn sleeping bags, books, notebooks, and various articles of clothing. As we walked around, my father picked a book up from the floor, Howard Fast's *My Glorious Brothers,* about the Maccabean revolt.

"I hoped to find something by Shalom Aleichem or Agnon in a camp for Jewish youngsters," he said in a disappointed tone. "You think young people read my books too?" he asked.

I couldn't answer him. In the distance, he spotted a red binding and thought he recognized one of his books. He picked it up; it was Hermann Hesse's *Narcissus and Goldmund.* A ladybug landed on the open book, and when his hand approached it, the insect spread its wings and hopped on his finger.

"You really think such a splendid creature is the product of evolution? All that talk about 'original mists' or the 'big bang' is nonsense. Of all the views about the creation of the world, the one in the Book of Genesis is the most correct," he said. "Darwin and Karl Marx didn't discover the secrets of the universe."

The camp guard appeared suddenly in patched overalls and heavy leather boots. He was an old farmer, short, with broad shoulders; his nose was red from drinking. He remembered me from the summer camp, and we were glad to see each other. I introduced him to my father, secretly hoping that he might have heard of him. But he hadn't. He had never heard of the Nobel Prize either. He apologized for not having had time to clean up the junk the "spoiled kids" had left. My father seemed pleased to be in the country.

We walked to the nearby town and managed to find a vegetarian restaurant. The waiter, a man in his seventies, started examining my father. Another pest, I thought, who had identified my father and would soon ask for an autograph. I pulled out a pen in anticipation. After looking at him furtively, my father suddenly exclaimed in Yiddish: "Zelig, what are you doing here?"

The waiter looked at my father and roared with joy: "Isaac!" They embraced.

"Zelig, remember when we were maybe eight or nine, you told me that the Jews had no future and the surest way to survive was to be like the Gentiles?"

"Of course I remember," he replied. "We were sitting in a tree, but you didn't want to convert to Christianity. And all by myself, it wasn't nice."

"So, did you convert?"

"What do you mean? Too late. Today, Isaac, the Jews have their own state. So what's the point in assimilation? Isaac, you know, my son lives in Tel Aviv, and every year I go visit him," he said proudly.

"My son's also in Israel, on a kibbutz," replied my father, introducing me. They spent the rest of the meal reliving their past.

When I returned to Israel, President Yitzhak Navon asked me whether my father would come on an official visit. Prime Minister Menachem Begin had insulted him some time ago on television in New York, and I wasn't sure that he'd agree to come. But I suggested that they invite him. To my surprise, my father accepted. When the news of his visit came out, institutions such as the World Jewish Congress, Shalom Aleichem House, the Yiddish Department at Hebrew University, organizations of immigrants from Bilgoray and Radzimin, and his friends in the Writers' Club of Warsaw, along with many other groups, joined the organizing committee. President Navon, sensing that things were getting out of hand, appointed a small committee, which included me, to organize the visit. Our mission was to avoid the political arena, and above all, the visit shouldn't be too much of a burden for the elderly author. But as the date approached, it became increasingly difficult to balance all the demands of the various factions and groups. Some organizations bypassed us and wrote to my father directly, complaining that they had been discriminated against.

We sent him the schedule we had prepared, and he immediately complained that the committee hadn't left him a minute to pee in peace. He wanted time to see some of his friends. Then, about a week before he was to arrive, he found out that one of the people welcoming him would be the Prime Minister Menachem Begin, and he canceled his visit on the spot. He called the writer Natan Shaham, asking him to inform the president that he wouldn't come. President Navon asked me to intervene. When I entered the president's office, I found him in a rage. He considered my father's refusal an insult to the state of Israel. I called my father from the president's office and tried to persuade him to change his mind, but he remained steadfast.

"I don't want to shake hands with the prime minister," he stated. "Maybe I'll come when you've got another prime minister who doesn't despise Yiddish."

This entire conflict dated back to a dreadful confrontation between him and the Israeli prime minister in New York. Menachem Begin had come to New York a few days before my father was to leave for Stockholm and asked to meet with him. Even though my father was terribly pressed for time, he agreed, asking the prime minister's staff to send a car for him. My father was told to get there on his own, which of course he regarded as a gross discourtesy. I urged him to go anyway, and ordered him a taxi. When he returned, my father said that their meeting had begun with a friendly conversation. But to my father's astonishment, soon into the visit, Begin told him that Yiddish would never be like Hebrew. It was impossible to give an order to a soldier in that language. How could you run an army in Yiddish? he asked. My father replied that Yiddish wasn't meant for running an army, Yiddish was a language of peace. He was insulted by the prime minister's deprecation of Yiddish just when it had achieved universal recognition, thanks to him. He so regarded Yiddish that he had felt it appropriate to open his speech in Stockhom in that very language. My father never forgave Begin and in fact never visited Israel again.

At the beginning of the Lebanese War in 1982, I met Prime Minister Begin. We were in the north, at the "Good Neighbors' Fence" near Metulla. As soon as he saw me he asked: "Mr. Zamir, how is your father?"

"Fine," I replied.

"Still mad at me?"

"Prime Minister, my father won't come to Israel as long as you're prime minister."

"There was exaggerated sensitivity and unfortunate misunderstanding on the part of your father back then, Mr. Zamir. After all, you're talking about an important Yiddish writer, but the state of Israel today confronts a new historical period," he said very solemnly. "Mr. Zamir, we are about to change the map of the Middle East. We are making a peace treaty with another Arab state, with Lebanon, after we help the Christians take over the government."

He was very excited and waved at the tank drivers on their way to Beirut.

22

THE GENERAL AND THE WRITER

During the eighties, on one of my New York visits, my father invited me to the famous Grossinger's Hotel in the Catskills. We left together in a limousine and enjoyed one of our most relaxed times traveling from the Bronx to the north.

"Did you ever wonder why the seed of that particular tree struck root while a seed that dropped not far from it remained barren? Didn't the two of them get the same rain? Is it just an accident?" he asked, pointing at a large tree by the road.

"A seed that drops on fertile ground has a better chance of sprouting than a seed that falls on a rock or on parched ground," I offered.

My father shook his head. Rational arguments never carried much weight with him. He went on watching the trees. "They look erect as cadets in a review."

"Cadets in a review! Do you have any idea what a cadet looks like? I bet you've never seen a row of cadets," I said.

He laughed and told me that he had once been invited to lecture at West Point.

"You, at West Point?!" I interrupted. It was hard to imagine. "What was a Jew like you doing at a military academy? You can't have found any Yiddish readers there! Did any of those cadets ever hear of your work?"

He told me that as the limousine was taking him and Alma to the lecture, he was gripped with doubt and kept asking himself all the way: what could I talk about with those Gentiles? My father had absolutely no experience or notion of weapons or military procedures and had never even gone through basic training. A two-thousand-dollar honorarium "wasn't so easy to come by in those days," he pointed out to me somewhat apologetically.

Upon reaching the military academy, my father was impressed to be greeted by a general with a Ph.D. from Princeton, whose family had come to America during the religious persecutions of the last century. Despite his apprehension, my father was touched by the reception he received and remarked that only in America could the grandson of a refugee get to be a general; in Europe, traditionally, he would have to have been born into the nobility to make a career in the military.

My father became very tense, he said, when the general informed him that the students of the academy were about to hold a review in his honor. Did this mean that he would have to salute? he inquired nervously. His host laughed and asked if my father had ever served in an army and if he had ever actually learned how to salute. My father shook his head and admitted to the general that several decades ago, back in Poland, after being drafted, he had fasted for several days, hoping not to be inducted into Marshal Pilsudski's anti-Semitic army. It worked.

Later that afternoon, my father and Alma were escorted by the general to an enormous parade ground filled with soldiers and cadets in full dress uniform. The cadets' uniforms, the general explained, had been designed at the beginning of the nineteenth century. The cadets marched in to the music of a band, their polished shoes and buckles flashing in the setting sun. "It was a great show. The field looked like a gigantic chessboard with tiny soldiers set up for war on it," my father remembered.

The general invited him to accompany him down to the parade ground. The cadets began to march. The general glanced at my father, who seemed bewildered. "Mr. Singer, please, don't worry about a thing," said the general, trying to reassure my father.

"So there I stood, a Jewish schlemiel out of place, a complete stranger to those bright swords, representative of a dying language that didn't mean a thing to anyone there. I was really embarrassed: the units of cadets filed by us, their heads turned to us on command, saluting sharply and rhythmically. Here they were, these proper, good-looking, clean-cut young Americans saluting a Yiddish writer who couldn't help himself from thinking at that very moment: Am I awake? Is this really happening to me?"

Closing his eyes a moment, my father continued: "And standing there with the units marching by and everyone's eyes on us, the religious judge, Rabbi Mendel Pinkhas, my own father, suddenly appeared in my mind's eye and stood on my right. He wore a *kapote* and a broad-brimmed hat, a *shtrayml,* with his unruly beard, his earlocks flying in the wind, trembling in fear at the authorities. On my left stood my witty and down-to-earth mother Bath Sheba, watching the whole thing like an absurd vision and trying with all her might not to burst out laughing."

He didn't dare disturb the military review. The old rabbi Pinkhas stood there erect, "trying, maybe, to represent as best he could an upright, proud Jew." At that moment, the Princeton Ph.D. whispered the names of the units passing by into his ear, which exacerbated his feeling of being out of place, out of time. The parade ended without incident, and the Singers, together with the general and a few other officials, went on to share a good dinner.

After dinner, they were escorted to the lecture hall. My father told me that throughout the visit he kept referring to the general as "doctor"; somehow, he had trouble pronouncing the word "general." The lecture went very well; he read his prepared text, lifting his head and glancing at the cadets from time to time, while they sat stiffly, gazing at him glassy-eyed. They probably hadn't the remotest idea what my father was talking about. With their hats neatly kept on their knees, they stared at him with blank faces. Sometimes he would slip in a few Jewish jokes and was disappointed when they didn't respond, as did most of his audiences, with an amused chuckle. What the cadets didn't know was that he was as scared and puzzled by them as they were by him.

The lecture ended. Then followed the customary question and answer period. My father was usually very sharp, having honed his answers for years. Someone asked how the hero of *Enemies, a Love Story* could live with three women at the same time. Grateful that someone had read one of his books, my father tried to explain that "such a thing can happen to any one of us." Another cadet asked him what he thought of Israel. My father replied that, for hundreds of years in Poland, Gentiles had hated Jews and had told them to go to Palestine. Some of them did, said my father, but when they got there, these Polish Jews were not welcome in Palestine and were asked to return unceremoniously to Poland, Germany, Spain. What were they to do? Where should they have gone? my father asked. Then something unusual occurred: he didn't know how to conclude the session. Pondering a moment, raising his head, and struggling to find his words, he was finally unable to think of anything better to say and wished them peace on earth and no more war. A rather inappropriate blessing, to be sure.

"There were quite a few embarrassing moments during my visit to West Point."

When we reached Grossinger's, unlike at West Point, my father felt very much at home among the mostly Yiddish-speaking Jews there.

23

NEW YORK SPEAKS YIDDISH

A big gala had been organized in Tel Aviv for the opening of the film *Yentl*. Those who could afford to pay $250 to see the film based on my father's play and have supper with the producer-director-screenwriter-actress-singer Barbra Streisand had gathered at a cinema in Tel Aviv. I attended the event, and when the film was over, I wanted to meet the actress. The security guards were fierce and blocked all the aisles to her chair. When I pleaded with one of the guards, explaining that my father was Bashevis Singer, he pushed me and replied angrily: "I don't know no Bashevis. Eliahu's the only one who gives orders here." So much for my wanting to shake hands with a real movie star. I left for home disappointed.

As a child my father first heard of the theater as he walked to the synagogue in Warsaw with his father, Reb Pinkhas. "That house is a den of thieves." His father grimaced in contempt, pointing to the theater. "Evil dwells there. Sinners go there, wanton women, and pig eaters."

Despite his longing to see what was going on in that "den of thieves," my father didn't set foot in a theater until he was twenty-four years old. He shaved off his earlocks and began going to the Yiddish theater in Warsaw, which presented original plays by such giants of Yiddish literature as Mendele mocher sforim, Shalom Aleichem, and I. L. Peretz, along with classics by dramatists such as Shakespeare, Strindberg, and Ibsen. But his first significant encounter with the theater occurred later, in 1935. On his way from Poland to America, he stopped in Paris, where he saw a production of *Yoshe Kalb,* based on the book by his brother I. J. Singer, and starring the famous Yiddish actor Morris Schwartz.

By the time he arrived in the United States, the American Yiddish theater was in decline. Most Yiddish authors in America didn't write for the stage, and theater owners had to translate material from English or compromise on "garbage," as my father put it. The standard Yiddish play featured a rich old Jew who wants to marry a poor virgin. Her tormented true lover can't rescue the girl from the clutches of the old man. In the end, of course, the young couple runs off to America, the land of freedom and happy endings. Another typical play was about a Polish or Russian estate owner in constant conflict with the Orthodox Jews under his protection, who manage to get around him and avoid violating the Torah. Such a play usually included lighting Sabbath candles and reciting the blessing over the wine, along with other common rituals. Jews who had recently come to America and missed their shtetl would flock to the Yiddish theater after a day of backbreaking toil in the sweatshops of Lower Manhattan. There they were able to commune with their memories.

When my father arrived in New York, his brother advised him that if he was at all serious about writing plays, he had better do it fast, because the Yiddish theater was on the verge of disappearing.

I wanted to see where the theater had been, and my father took me downtown, to lower Second Avenue. What I saw was a run-down theater showing dirty movies. I looked inside; the plaster was peeling off the walls. That had been the Yiddish theater in the 1930s, the place where Jews came from all over the city for their entertainment. The liquor shop next to the theater had once been a cafeteria where the actors and the audience would meet after the show. But those days when downtown New York spoke mainly Yiddish were long gone. So was the Yiddish theater.

We stood there watching the winos and the strange mix of people around us. Beggars haggled with my father. They were apparently dissatisfied with the quarter he had given them. A Salvation Army band of Irish women played psalms on their trumpets, and a preacher in glorious apparel urged the drunks to return to Jesus. They listened dully, waiting patiently for a handout that would allow them to return to the liquor shop.

My father's play *Yentl, a Yeshiva Boy* was first performed at the O'Neill Theater on Broadway in 1975, when my father was seventy-one years old. I wondered why he had waited so long, and he explained that if Robert Kaplan of the Chelsea Theater hadn't suggested that he adapt *Yentl* as a play, he probably wouldn't have done it on his own. A play should be written originally as a play, he kept saying, and not be based on a story, which, in his opinion, lost a lot of its artistic value in the process. The great playwrights — Shakespeare, Molière, Ibsen, Strindberg — composed their works as plays from the start. Dramatizing a story is possible, but what's impossible is to turn a play into a story.

" 'You can turn chicken soup into beet borscht, but you can't turn beet borscht into chicken soup,' my Aunt Yentl used to say."

Despite his fascination with the theater, for most of his life, my father hesitated to write plays. A play earned its author incomparably higher royalties than stories, he said, and he often

talked about writing for the stage. *Schlemiel the First,* based on
the Chelm stories, and *Devil's Play,* based on his "invisible"
stories, were two of my father's plays. They were performed
off-Broadway but were not successful and soon closed. The two
plays *Yentl* and *Taybele and the Demon,* however, did bring him
fame. *Yentl* was later put on Broadway and played for more than
two hundred performances. The actress Tova Feldshuh, who
played Yentl, was very successful. She integrated with great
finesse a femininity with an ardor to study the Talmud. When
my father's theater success made people aware that his stories
could be adapted to the stage, he was besieged by many pro-
ducers. Both stage and screen rights to his books and short
stories were bought, thus providing an unexpected additional
source of income.

But my father's experience with film was not altogether
happy. Barbra Streisand, who had bought the film rights to
Yentl, rejected his screenplay and wrote her own script. She had
paid a good deal for the film rights and felt that she could do
what she pleased with the original material. Her film was a
profound disappointment to my father. Ms. Streisand, who
controlled the entire production, managed to appear in every
scene. Her constant singing throughout the film annoyed my
father: "If she wants to sing, that's her right," he remarked. "But
why should Yentl have to suffer?" In my father's story, Yentl isn't
a girl with musical aspirations but one who wants to study the
Torah, a girl with the soul of a scholar. And that's why she
disguises herself as a boy. Streisand's Yentl is a girl seeking
happiness. What happiness? America. Did she sail there to study
the Torah? If it's studying Torah you want, the yeshivas of
Poland and Lithuania are better. "There's too much singing in
the film and too little Torah," he commented dejectedly. "My
Yentl wasn't interested in the women's liberation movement so

popular in the United States; she didn't even burn her bra." The ending also made him very angry: "That's how a screenwriter can send Raskolnikov from *Crime and Punishment* to the New York stock market instead of Siberia. Or imagine Anna Karenina, instead of committing suicide, marrying a real estate agent from Chicago," he said. "And what will Yentl do in America? She'll live on the Lower East Side, work in a sweatshop for fourteen hours a day to support herself. And when will she study the Torah? Or maybe Streisand means for her Yentl to end up like all the other women in the Bronx who go to the Jewish Center every Tuesday to play bingo? The end of the movie exposes all its weaknesses," he continued. "Her personal sacrifice and her longing to study the Torah were replaced by the American dream." He was very upset about it and considered the screenplay shallow and unimaginative — a superficial, commercial musical comedy. He wrote a furious article about it for the *New York Times*. Predictably, thousands flocked to the film, hoping to figure out why the author was so enraged.

Another experience with the cinema was when director Paul Mazursky visited my father in Miami Beach before filming *Enemies, a Love Story*. Mazursky found the writer looking frail in a wheelchair by the swimming pool at his apartment building. My father gazed at him dully as he entered and without any preamble said: "I didn't like what Barbra Streisand did to *Yentl*."

Mazursky promised that there wouldn't be any songs in his film, which greatly reassured my father. He then showed him pictures of the actors he had selected, and when my father saw the picture of Lena Olin, who had been cast to play the part of Masha, he smiled and predicted that the film would be a success. Mazursky asked my father: "Mr. Singer, are you Herman?"

He smiled: "We're all Herman. The minute a man marries a woman, he starts looking for a mistress."

My father's Herman is indeed a skirt chaser, but he's also an intellectual whose views deepen his character and explain his feelings. In the book, he's a man haunted by nightmares, a victim of Nazi atrocities, on an endless search for the meaning of life. In the film, however, his philosophical view of life disappears, and you have a haunted victim fleeing from his wife to his lusty mistress and then back to his wife Tamara, who suddenly returns from hell. In one passage of the book, Herman says:

> Religions lied. Philosophy was bankrupt from the beginning. The idle promises of progress were no more than a spit in the face of the martyrs of all generations. If time is just a form of perception, or a category of reason, the past is as present as today. . . . Jews are forever being burned in Auschwitz. Those without courage to make an end to their existence have only one other way out: to deaden their consciousness, choke their memory, extinguish the last vestige of hope.

Such musings were not expressed in the film, and in my opinion, the character emerged as shallow.

My father didn't like any of the films made from his books. "When a man writes a book," he explained, "he is in total control of the material. It is he who decides what the hero will say, what he'll wear, what he'll think, and how many lines he'll devote to every problem. His work is in his hands like clay in the hands of the Creator. But when the film director takes control of a written work, he changes it and usually lowers it to the lowest common denominator so that the largest possible audience will go see the film."

He was convinced that all the films made from his works would turn out badly and concluded that his stories couldn't be made into movies. Their essence would be lost in the process. Because his health wasn't up to it, my father didn't see the film version of *Enemies, a Love Story.* Sometime later he asked me if I had seen the film *The Magician of Lublin,* also based on his book. Did I remember how the book ends? I described the end to him: Yasha Mazor returns to the faith and locks himself in a solitary cell.

"Right. And you remember how the film ends?"

"I do."

"Real filth," he spat out in disgust.

24

GOD IS UNFAIR TO LIFE

In the summer of 1986, I was staying at the Village Hotel near Washington Square. People seemed to be running every hour of the day in that park. There were thousands of them jogging endlessly around and around the square, day in and day out. Had he been a thirty-year-old man, my father said, he would no doubt have joined in and jogged along with everyone: "Running is America at its best." During one of his many interviews, my father was asked what New York meant to him; he replied with a single word: "Rush."

I decided one morning to participate in the ritual of running around the square. I found it pleasant and soon realized that I was running behind a short black man with a red band around his forehead and a big crucifix on his chest. Every now and then he looked back at me suspiciously. Whether he sped up or slowed down, I was on his heels. After we had run around the square for some time, he stopped and asked abruptly: "Mister, how come you're following me?"

"What do you mean, following you?"

"For God's sake, why don't you run around me when I slow down?"

I shrugged and smiled.

He glanced at me suspiciously but soon realized that I didn't mean any harm. "OK, let's take a break and sit down on a bench," he said.

Before sitting down, he pulled a roll of paper out of his pocket and spread it out on the bench. That surprised me, and I told him so.

"God sends millions of AIDS germs here. You see that guy sleeping on the bench?" He pointed to a thin, bearded fellow covered with a piece of cardboard and a tattered sleeping bag. "Infected with AIDS. His family threw him out of the house so he wouldn't infect them. He's been living here in the square for a long time now, until the Creator takes his soul."

We got into a conversation about running, what it does for the body and the soul. Then I asked a question about his private life: "What do you do for a living?"

He looked at me, licked his lips, and asked: "Hey, man, you a pig or a detective or something?"

"Of course not," I replied. "Just interested, that's all."

He thought for a moment, uncertain whether he should continue, and finally he said: "I'll tell you, but only if you don't turn me in, OK?"

"OK."

"During the day, I'm studying to be a minister. I'm in my last year of divinity school. And at night, I'm a pickpocket." He looked me over and added: "Hey, man, don't keep your wallet in your back pocket. There's nothing easier than lifting it from there." As he spoke, his thin fingers seemed to move by themselves. I was very impressed by his candor.

"Isn't there a contradiction between your two occupations, or professions?" I asked.

"God knows my business. As a minister, I pray a lot and He

forgives a lot. Give and take. Sometimes there's a misunderstanding, like in any good family."

"My father was recently mugged," I told him.

"Where?"

"On Broadway."

"Hey, man, Broadway is a very long street."

"Near 86th Street."

"Not my turf. I work from 14th to 23rd Street. Busy place.
Lots of supermarkets there. Lots of work."

I later told my father about that strange encounter, with its
combination of earthly and heavenly labor. He laughed and said
that all big cities in the world are divided among the members
of the underworld. In Warsaw, too, every neighborhood had its
own local thieves. The robbers of Gnoina and Krochmalna even
had their own peculiar smell of herring and vodka.

"If I were thrown into that area today, blindfolded, I'd know
at once where I was. On the square on Krochmalna Street, a lot
of thieves, gamblers, and prostitutes used to congregate. Every
quarter had a 'boss,' a kind of 'One Who Makes Peace in His
Heaven,' whose decisions were irrevocable. New York, Moscow, London, Warsaw, it's all the same everywhere. By the way,
you say that the black man you met works downtown. I better
warn Alma." And he added that God created heaven and earth
so we wouldn't get bored.

The next day, my father met with Yelena Bonner, wife of
Andrey Sakharov — Russian scientist, Nobel Peace Prize winner, and Soviet dissident. Mrs. Bonner had come to New York
for medical treatment. She had read some of my father's books
and short stories that had been translated and distributed in the
Soviet underground. She looked very Jewish, he said. She told
my father that he had many admirers in the Soviet Union and
praised him. He felt uncomfortable about that, especially after

hearing that she had cut his picture out of an American magazine and hung it in her house. He was used to compliments, of
course, but Yelena Bonner's words were particularly moving to
him. My father hoped that they wouldn't suffer any more evil in
the Soviet Union and told her that he prayed to God to protect
them. He was conscious of the importance of this momentous
visit.

Yelena Bonner asked my father whether he was religious. In
his own way, he replied. He didn't follow any particular religious observance. He believed in God and was sure that God
was with us every moment of our lives. He also told her that he
was a vegetarian: "If it's forbidden to slaughter a person, for me,
it's also forbidden to wring a chicken's neck," he explained. She
told him that in Russia, she had often prepared a Jewish feast of
fruit and vegetables on Friday night. Once, as she and her
husband sat to enjoy their meal, her husband had asked her with
a smile: "Do you want to turn me into Isaac Bashevis Singer?"

My father greatly admired her husband and praised him as an
extraordinarily brave man. Sakharov, in my father's opinion,
had to be a believer, for behind his courage there was an ardent
belief, he told her. Whether it was a belief in God or in
humanism or in anything else, for that matter, the great Soviet
scientist had lived like a man of faith, even though my father
deplored belief in humanism and found it disappointing. "Of all
the lies in the world, humanism is the biggest. Humanism
doesn't serve one idol but all the idols. They were all humanists:
Mussolini, Hitler, Stalin," he wrote in *The Penitent*.

My father paid tribute to Yelena Bonner; he regarded her as a
woman of valor, a woman of action, and told her so. As for him,
he was merely a man of words, and actions, he continued, were
infinitely more important than words. "But words are actions,"
she said. "You don't know what comes first — the word or the

act." They talked for a little while longer, and when they parted, she promised that if she ever returned to New York she would come back and visit him.

"How can a person like you claim to believe in God yet live a completely secular life?" I repeatedly asked him.

"With your father, everything's possible," Alma answered for him.

"You must know that we've already been in this world before," commented my father, tracking a fly buzzing around a lightbulb. "Because, as far as God is concerned, it doesn't make sense for Him to send a soul into the world only once. Maybe in a previous incarnation, I was a rabbi somewhere. Because the fact is that my tongue constantly rattles around verses and sayings of our Sages of Blessed Memory, which I know without ever having studied them. Can you explain the world without God? Whenever I'm in trouble, I look up at the sky and pray. Since I'm in trouble most of the time, I never stop praying. Not a regular prayer from the prayer book. A personal conversation between me and the Creator. Mostly I plead with Him, but sometimes I also complain. I often told Him that I don't justify His acts. Not a day goes by without a sharp dialogue between us. In many cases, He responds to my prayers and gives answers to my distress. Sometimes the plot of my story is stuck like a cart in the mud, and I don't know how to get it out. I prostrate myself, hesitate, sometimes put in a prayer to Him, and suddenly a heavenly illumination, and the cart slides out of the swampy mud. The belief that man is the master of his fate is as far from me as east is from west. God is silent, speaks in acts; and we on earth have to decipher His secrets. We long for faith as much as we yearn for sex. Our great hope is free choice, divine gift. I suppose that that robber you met in Washington Square will get to the seat of judgment someday and stand before his fate."

"Like you, he makes a distinction between his belief in the Creator of the world on the one hand, and everyday life on the other."

"I don't rob people."

"I didn't say you did. Yet I can't understand your God, who ignored the Holocaust. So many Hasids and saints were led to the gas chambers, not for any crime they committed. And as they went, they recited the *Shema,* the credo of the Jewish faith."

"Son, we can't understand everything. God, apparently, promises but isn't in much of a hurry to keep His word. He promised the Land of Israel to the Jews and it took about two thousand years from the time He made the promise until the people won the land. From His point of view, maybe that's not very long. I've often told you that although I believe in God and admire His divine wisdom, I can't praise Him for His mercy. Sometimes I long to go out in the street and picket God with a big poster saying: God Is Unfair to Life! All the problems of divine belief can be boiled down to one question: why is there suffering? And the answer is that without suffering, there is no belief."

I recalled those words four years later when my wife and I were sent to the Soviet Union to teach Hebrew in Lwów. When I came back, I told my father about Russia, where religion had been outlawed, where churches had been turned into youth clubs and synagogues into warehouses. After more than seventy years of communist brainwashing, religious faith in Russia is on the increase, and a great many people are returning to the churches.

"When we got to Lwów, the great synagogue was still standing, forlorn. For more than fifty years, it had been used as a warehouse to store bottles. They did everything they could to wipe out the Jewish religion. Zhidowska Ulitsa, 'Jew Street,' had been changed to Serispkaya Ulitsa. At the entrance to the Rapoport Jewish Maternity Hospital, a statue of the anti-Semitic Ukrainian poet Shbchanko had been erected. None of the expectant Soviet mothers ever knew that it had originally been a Jewish hospital."

"That country can't last very long," my father predicted. "How long can you oppress a people and steal their cultural and spiritual treasures? You can't uproot belief."

We had gone to Brody, I told him, the city where the Council of Four Lands had once convened, and where two-thirds of the inhabitants had been Jews.

"Brody was a very famous Jewish town," my father commented. "Are there any Jews left there?"

"I asked passersby if there were any Jews, and somebody remembered Semyon Semyonovitch, a peddler in the city market — the last Jew in Brody."

Semyon was quite moved when we went to his house. He had never met any Jews from Israel. Born in Brody, he had fled east and joined the Red Army when World War II broke out. When he returned at the end of the war, he didn't find a single Jew in the town. He discovered his mother's tombstone in the Jewish cemetery. In time, he married, had a son, and, like everyone else, lived in a crowded apartment. He had been hiding a Torah scroll all those years in the wardrobe; the scroll had been partially burned when the Germans had set fire to the synagogue. A Ukrainian friend of his had found it and given it to him. After carefully checking to make sure that the door was locked and the shutters closed tight, he pulled a scroll with scorched edges out of the closet. With trembling hands, he unrolled it and kissed it. I saw tears in his eyes.

"This is all that's left of Brody Jewry," he said.

My father shook his head sadly. I stopped talking; we both remained silent. "Semyon asked us to go with him to the old Jewish cemetery," I continued. "On the way, he pointed to a big house that had once been a Jewish theater. 'That was the old people's home, and over there was the synagogue where the famous rabbi of Anateka prayed.' We didn't find any remnant of a Jewish community in Brody. The cemetery was on a hill outside the town. About twenty thousand Jews from Brody had been gathered and destroyed in May 1943. Semyon led us to his mother's grave, brushed some dry leaves off the tombstone, and began reciting the kaddish. He glanced around, as if afraid that the stones would hear. For years he hadn't dared visit his mother's grave for fear of the Ukrainians. He would break off his prayer from time to time because he was all choked up. The cemetery is covered with weeds, the stones are mossy, and the inscriptions are blurred. The stones are sinking and no one is restoring them. The cemetery itself is being buried," I concluded.

"I'm very familiar with the stories of the pogroms of 1648 and 1649," my father responded. "I often said that God was indifferent during the Holocaust, sat there in His Seventh Heaven, surrounded by angels singing loud hymns of praise and glory to Him. The Jews cried out from the ovens, the crematoria, but He didn't hear. While He was getting praise, we got the gas chambers."

25

SALUTE TO IMMIGRANTS

It was summer 1986. The day was July 4. All through New York, celebrations commemorating the hundredth anniversary of the Statue of Liberty, symbol of immigration to this country, were being held. Like so much in America, even this celebration seemed commercialized to me. People walked around the city with plastic wreaths on their heads, symbolizing Lady Liberty's crown. Cotton shirts, jeans, coats — everything bore the logo of the statue. Even in bakeries, I found rolls in the shape of the statue. The poem of the Jewish author Emma Lazarus at the base of the Statue of Liberty was turned into a jingle, played incessantly on radio and television. The White House was going to honor a dozen immigrants for "their unique contribution to the United States of America." But New York Mayor Ed Koch, feeling that that didn't really represent the waves of immigrants that had flooded this continent or the distinguished refugees of New York, decided to hold his own separate ceremony.

Macy's placed an enormous ad in the *New York Times* (every event in America, I was told, has to have a sponsor) announcing that the city would salute eighty-seven famous American citizens who had immigrated to New York from fifty countries:

"They have found a warm home here and they adorn the city and improve its quality — a pattern and a model of the profound meaning of freedom." One of the honored guests was my father, and he invited me to come along with him.

It was July, and New York was very hot. The ceremony was held at the southern tip of Manhattan, near Battery Park, at the site of a U.S. Navy memorial to fallen sailors. For the U.S. Navy, this ceremony was very important.

A cadet escorted my father to the special platform for the honorees, while a military band played loud marches. The families were seated underneath. Under this blazing sun, the former immigrants were sweating profusely and wiping their faces. They quickly became friendly with one another, and everyone was chatting amiably. But for some reason — probably because of the heat — that day my father kept to himself, not exchanging a word with anyone.

The other honored guests included such notables as science fiction writer Isaac Asimov, film director and writer Elia Kazan, Australian newspaper magnate Rupert Murdoch, Irish actress Maureen O'Hara, Irish-Mexican actor Anthony Quinn, and blind Indian writer Ved Mehta.

As the pianist played the opening of "The Star Spangled Banner," everyone rose. Ed Koch put his hand over his heart, flags flew, swords were pulled out of their sheaths and gleamed in the bright sunshine. As we all waited for the singing to begin, it was discovered that the famous opera singer Kiri Te Kanawa hadn't arrived. She was nowhere in sight. The microphone was standing by itself; the pianist backstage, assuming that the singer hadn't heard the opening bars, kept repeating them over and over. No one had bothered to tell him that the singer hadn't shown up. A few long, hot moments passed.

People ran around while the mayor waved his arms nervously and issued orders to his assistants. The audience, which had stood up, sat down.

Here was America, I thought, dressed to the nines, prepared down to the last detail, and it can't get its act together. Off in the distance, as if rising from a bath, pure and shining, was the hundred-year-old Lady Liberty. Maybe she was smiling to herself at this screwup. This was a celebration of immigrants, and they had never been known for their order and precision.

About half an hour later, Kiri Te Kanawa finally appeared. Without waiting for the opening bars of the piano, she rushed to the microphone and belted out the national anthem, fortissimo. Everyone scrambled to his feet. The officers saluted, the cadets pulled out their swords again, the politicians clapped their hands over their hearts, and everyone joined in the singing.

Mayor Ed Koch went to the microphone: "You see? There was a breakdown. The singer couldn't make her way through the traffic jam, but in the end everything worked out, because in America we succeed in the end, 'cause that's America!" he called out in excitement. The sun was blazing, and the honored guests were grumbling and groaning. A traffic jam in Upper Manhattan had thwarted a detailed program. The schedule had been completely disrupted. The mayor cut short his welcome but didn't abandon his opening remarks:

> Honored guests, as mayor of New York, I govern more Jews than there are in Jerusalem, more blacks than there are in Nairobi, more Irish than there are in Dublin, more Puerto Ricans than there are in San Juan, and more Italians than there are in Firenze. If you live in New York and miss your hometown, it

doesn't mean that you're foreign, but that you live in the wrong neighborhood.

Smiles and applause. It was noon, and the sun was hopelessly frying all of us. The crowd was growing impatient. I looked at my father. His fair-skinned face was glistening with sweat. His head was bent as if he had fallen asleep. He was sure that he was being punished for some sin and that Satan had locked him in an oven, condemned to burn, he told me later. He knew that Satan does the work of the Holy-One-Blessed-Be-He, and my father sat there waiting for his fate, still and chastened.

The great moment finally arrived: the honorees were going to be awarded medals. The person's name was read off, and a pair of sailors in navy blue and white marched to the honoree, saluted, and hung the medal around his or her neck, as everyone applauded. The names of eighty-seven persons were read, and the naval crews worked quickly and efficiently. When the naval cadets saluted him, my father was moved — he, the representative of the shtetl. When one of the cadets put a medal around his neck, he beamed with delight.

Everything might have ended all right had it not been for one of the winners, who, upon examining his medal, noticed that someone else's name was engraved on it. He rushed to the microphone and announced the mistake. Everyone took off his or her medal and discovered that no one had bothered to match the name on the medal with the person it belonged to. This began a nice scramble. The honorees ran around the platform, calling to one another, trying to get things straightened out. In the middle of all that turmoil, a choir burst into song. Fireworks were shot into the bright sky. It looked like sparks from a bonfire. A huge blimp passed in the sky with enormous letters:

Coca Cola. It covered the sun for a moment, and everyone breathed a quick sigh of relief.

"Give me your tired and poor Coca Cola," someone sitting behind me recited, parodying the Emma Lazarus poem on the Statue of Liberty.

The embarrassed master of ceremonies asked everyone to kindly return the medals to him, insisting that he would redistribute them. The steamed assembly didn't move; people seemed glued to their chairs with sweat. Then as the choir went on singing, the honored guests began leaving.

My father didn't seem upset about it. He took off the medal, glanced at the name on it — Liv Ullmann — and laughed, adding that he was a fan of hers and thought that she was beautiful. He'd put it in his archive, a room where everything was tossed at random — books, newspapers, tributes, honorary doctorates, and medals. (I once brought him a document and a brass tablet that named him a "Notable of the Diaspora Museum" in Tel Aviv. After glancing at it, he asked me to "put it in the attic." There was no attic in his apartment. By attic, we all knew that he meant the messy room in the back, where he assumed that all his treasures would be discovered after his death.)

As we were leaving, Ed Koch shook my father's hand warmly, hugged him, and said: "Mr. Singer, it is an honor and a pleasure for me that you, a resident of our city, graced this ceremony with your presence. There were disruptions, but that shouldn't obscure the joy. President Reagan invited a dozen well-known immigrants to the White House, and, in my opinion, you should have been the first to be invited."

Obviously pleased, my father smiled and replied: "Mr. Mayor, I thank you, but I have no desire to go to Washington. Your medal, as a Jewish mayor who speaks and knows Yiddish, is infinitely more important to me than the medal of a goy from the West."

After we got back to his apartment and had cooled off in his air-conditioned living room, I was interested to know what he had thought of the ceremony — aside from suffering from the heat.

"You may not believe me, but the statue took me back to my youth and my first days on this continent."

Back in Poland, when he was a boy, his mother used to read letters from America to people who could not read, and he would always listen. Many of the letters mentioned the Statue of Liberty, the evil immigration officials who interrogated those arriving on Ellis Island and spoke Yiddish to them, and the sweatshops and the difficulties. As a child, he didn't know what the word "statue" meant. In his imagination, he told me, he often traveled to America, where he had long conversations with the statue, who spoke Yiddish. For him, that statue symbolized light and freedom. The immigrants loved Lady Liberty, believing that as long as she stood there, there was hope for the tired and the poor.

During the ceremony, my father had glanced now and then affectionately at the statue. He also reflected on the failure of the American "melting pot." He thought about those first-generation immigrants, who, in an effort to better assimilate, wanted to do away with their past and their heritage. So many had shortened their last names and stayed away from the synagogue. The second and third generations understood that nothing was gained by obliterating the past; they returned to their language and culture. He also knew that many of them read his books.

Upon arriving in America, my father, like so many immigrants before him, was plagued by the problems of earning a living. His tourist visa had to be renewed every six months, and he lived with the constant danger of being deported. Everything was entangled "in the webs of bureaucracy, and the calendar was disrupted," he told me, "like at the mayor's ceremony." The Polish quota for the United States was full, and it was impossible to get a permanent visa. A Jewish lawyer suggested that he go to Detroit, cross the border illegally to Windsor, Canada, and request a visa from there. But neither country was eager to accede to his request. He remained in New York that hot summer, preparing documents and the replies he was expected to give when appearing in front of American immigration officials.

"In those days, I was one of the 'tired and poor,' the ones the poem on the Statue of Liberty invited to come here," he added. During that hot summer, in an effort to cool off, every day he paid a nickel to ride the Staten Island ferry. He remembered fondly the sea breeze that had refreshed him then and had been hoping that the same wind would blow during the ceremony.

"Back then, when I sailed, I used to ponder the contradiction between human situations and human laws. The idea that someday I might see the statue for the last time, that I'd be deported from this country, gave me fears and nightmares. I can't forget the anxieties of that hot summer. And I thought of all that during the ceremony. Perhaps the hot sun helped me in its own way."

The phone rang. It was the mayor's clerk, who was offering the mayor's apologies again for the mix-up at the ceremony. My father smiled and reassured her that mix-ups were acceptable and sometimes even good.

26

THE LAST SUPPER

I returned to New York after a two-year absence and found my father at home, dozing in his chair. He muttered something sleepily. His hands shook. A special watch to measure his pulse was attached to his wrist. He wore sneakers with Velcro fasteners. His once blue eyes were dark. One of them had recently been operated on, and he was still in pain. About a year before, his prostate had been removed. When he was in severe pain, he would explode in a fit of rage and shift his body around, seeking some relief. His mind was lucid, though, and he seemed glad to see me. I brought along my new translation, *The Penitent*. My father felt the paperback binding with his square fingers and expressed disappointment. The book was too thin for his taste, too much like a pamphlet, he complained.

"Why didn't they make the letters bigger to make the book thicker?" he asked. When he looked at the binding, he saw a picture of a Hasid hovering in the sky between New York and Israel, as the wind plays with his earlocks and the hem of his coat. He laughed and said that he liked the picture. "The Messiah won't come from New York," was his comment. He opened the book and tried to read it, but his eyes couldn't follow an entire line and slid down to the line beneath. He thought he had found some typos and got angry. I took the book from him and read it aloud, and my father soon understood that the fault had been with his eyes. He asked me to continue reading. As I read the first page, he looked satisfied.

He recalled his own visit to the Western Wall: A Sephardic rabbi dressed in white and surrounded by a circle of curious onlookers was preaching in Hebrew about the Messiah. Some visitors recited the mourner's prayer, and others chanted the Eighteen Benedictions; some wound phylacteries around their arms, others swayed over the Book of Psalms. Everyone wore skullcaps, even those who were clean shaven. Beggars held out hands for alms, some even haggling with their benefactors. The Almighty conducted business here on a twenty-four-hour basis.

My father was pleased with my translation into Hebrew; he smiled and kissed me, surprising me with his emotion.

We talked about Joseph Shapiro, the hero of *The Penitent,* who is fed up with America and loathes his wife, who is cheating on him. He travels to Tel Aviv only to discover that it is no different from New York. Upon visiting a kibbutz, he is surprised that people still bow to Moloch there, in the person of Joseph Stalin. Is Mea Shearim all that's left? I asked. My father nodded. If a person fled from secular life, he claimed, the only thing he could do was join the religious world. "There's no compromise between religious life and secular life," he said.

My father remarked that for hundreds of years Jews had chosen a religious life of their own free will. That was how our fathers and forefathers had lived for generations. My father personally didn't choose a religious life. Many Jews, however, did, and the number of penitents is increasing today. Penitence, he continued, isn't a rebellion against the pleasures of life but a rebellion against despair. "I'm not calling for penitence in that book. I describe the life of Joseph Shapiro, who is fed up with 'eat, drink, and be merry,' and apparently there are a lot like him. Literature doesn't deal with penitents as a social phenomenon. That's what sociology or psychology is about."

When the book appeared in Hebrew, I told him that some critics thought he was preaching penitence because he despaired of the secular world and wanted, in his old age, to return to his boyhood, the yeshiva, and the seminary. He smiled. He was familiar with the argument, was my father's comment. In his opinion, the life of modern man was burdened with a sense of alienation, one he had often wanted to escape. Mea Shearim is not a city of refuge; life there is very hard. To be a Sandzer Hasid is a full-time, twenty-four-hour-a-day job. Joseph Shapiro wanted to cut himself off from the ugliness and hypocrisy of New York and from the temptations of that city.

"Could Joseph Shapiro perhaps be Isaac Bashevis Singer?" I asked, quoting one of his critics.

He looked at me, angry. "Nonsense. You know me. You also know that I have never been a saint and never will be. Literature has a right to invent and describe characters and present a world from their point of view. There is only one Joseph Shapiro, the one I wrote about, and he's the only one who sees the world like that."

At that moment, his secretary Dvora Menashe came into the room. My father's face lit up; he was happy to see her. She brought him his mail, and he impatiently looked through the pile; he was interested in opening only the envelopes with checks in them. Dvora Menashe had come specifically to help Alma pack. She and my father were getting ready to leave for Miami Beach the next day.

Taking me aside, Alma said: "This time it will be a long stay.

Your father has stopped writing because of his pain. I'm hoping that the warm weather will be good for him."

My father called me close to him. He seemed anxious to resume our conversation. Ever since he had become sick, he seemed to be mainly absorbed with worries and the treatments administered to him. He hadn't been able to see his old friends or journalists, and he felt spiritually deflated and alienated. He no longer had the chance to express his opinions. I looked at my father, sitting somewhat diminished in his wheelchair, his trembling hand clutching the new Hebrew translation I had brought him, and for a moment I was overwhelmed by a great sadness.

No philosophical conclusions should be drawn from his book about the way a person makes life choices, my father said to me. Joseph Shapiro's decision concerns him alone. From his point of view, he was right to choose Mea Shearim. Meeting the student Priscilla on the plane to Israel had been enough for his protagonist to forget all his vows, for lust to overcome him, and for his hand to steal under her dress. Because of his weakness of character, it was imperative for Shapiro to live within strict boundaries. Man needed restrictions, external symbols, and needed to avoid temptation. Had Joseph Shapiro been wearing a *kapote* and a *shtrayml* on the plane, Priscilla probably wouldn't have started a conversation with him.

"I understand Joseph Shapiro's heart, but his way isn't mine. I've often despaired about the nonsense of this world and wanted to escape. I once told a group of students that my dream is to flee to Japan to a young geisha who would take care of me there. Jews always fled in search of happiness. Your communist mother and many like her fled to Russia, to the 'light of the nations,' and froze in Siberia. You were lucky you were thrown out of there. Joseph Shapiro flees too."

While speaking, my father would become short of breath,

and his talk would be interrupted by a coughing spell. All that verbal activity was more than his lungs could take. There were moments when all that came out was a mere whistle. His face was pale. His chest rose and fell rapidly. Alma asked us to stop talking. We fell silent. Out his window I could see the greenery in the courtyard. The trees were in full bloom, squirrels were running around merrily on the walls, and I watched children throwing nuts at them.

My father announced that he wanted to go out to eat. Unable to locate the key to the apartment, my father lamented that forgetfulness was increasingly gnawing at him. I had just bought an electronic key ring and explained that when you whistle, it's supposed to respond with loud beeps — which of course leads you to it. He looked at me with wonderment. Really? Pulling the toy out of my pocket, I gave it to him. He looked at it for several seconds and then said: "There has to be a demon inside it. It can't be that a mere whistle of mine will make this object beep back at me." Eager to demonstrate my new purchase and to prove to my father that no demon inhabited it, I went to the far end of the apartment and hid the key ring. I then returned to my father and whistled. When loud and clear beeping suddenly emanated from the other room, my father's face lit up, and he cheered like a child. He wanted to try, but unable to breathe sufficiently to whistle, my father clapped — this was the other option — hoping that that would trigger the beep. It didn't. He resumed looking for his key while carrying on a monologue about his books. Yes, he admitted, the heroes of his stories often disappeared abruptly, and his stories stopped as if arriving at a dead end. The desperate Herman of *Enemies, a Love Story* hides in a hayloft in New York; Yasha, *The Magician of Lublin*, goes off to a cage he built; Jacob, *The Slave*, finds no peace of mind after Wanda dies and goes to Eretz-Israel and back to Poland, where he kneels at his beloved's grave. As for Yentl, she disappears completely. Most of his endings are sad.

"No, I won't write a story about happiness. A happy man isn't material for literature. Such a man doesn't interest me in the least. Moments of happiness in a person are brief. He's mostly in great trouble. When I stood in Stockholm, in the splendid hall of the Swedish Royal Academy, and shook hands with the king of Sweden, even though at the moment I felt proud and happy, in my mind's eye, I already saw the next day when the jealous literary critics would pounce on my work."

We went to the American Restaurant on Broadway. Walking had become difficult for my father. In the street, people greeted my father, but it didn't give him any pleasure. The pigeons on Broadway no longer seemed to recognize him. As we were crossing the street, the light changed more quickly than we had anticipated, and a driver honked at us and shouted: "Mister, if you're a silly old fool and can't cross the street any faster, go back home!" Such a remark would previously have unleashed a tirade from my father, but he remained silent as he made his way to the other side of the street.

The restaurant owner, an old friend of his, hurried as usual to welcome my father and escorted us to his regular table in the back of the room. We sat down, and feeling his strength returning, my father, ignoring Alma's pleas to catch his breath, started talking again.

"No, we have no answer to how the world was created. Joseph Shapiro puts his faith in the Almighty. He thinks the world was created just as the Big Ben in London was created. If a clock isn't 'created by itself,' can such a complicated mechanism as mankind be created by itself? All that talk about 'explosions' or the 'big bang' twenty million years ago is an unproved assumption. Joseph Shapiro and I both believe that there's a plan for the world, that higher forces, whether you call them 'God' or 'Nature,' created it. Nothing is random."

I couldn't help but feel that this had the ring of a spiritual last will and testament.

He ordered his standard vegetarian dinner, which consisted of spinach cutlets, potatoes, and vegetable soup. He had always declared that the Torah regards eating meat as a human weakness, the pursuit of the "fleshpots." He went on at great length about sects in India that make vegetarianism part of their religion. Everything connected with the slaughter or flaying of an animal was loathsome to my father. His hero Joseph Shapiro was also a vegetarian, but in Mea Shearim, he was criticized for that: "You needn't be more saintly than the saints. You must not pity creatures more than the Almighty does." My father was connecting animal slaughter with human bloodshed and the lack of peace on earth. "There's only one step between 'Thou shalt not kill' and 'Thou shalt not slaughter,' " he said. He kept pleading with me over and over to become a vegetarian. We ate in silence for a while. I watched him looking at me, obviously wanting to speak. We both knew that this day might be our last visit. There was only a slight chance that we would see each other again in the future.

He finished eating. "In Israel, they attack Yiddish," he said. "Intellectuals, rabbis, professors, writers like I. L. Peretz, Mendele mocher sforim, Shalom Aleichem, Aharon Zeitlin spoke and wrote Yiddish, but in Israel they laugh at that language." He once again mentioned Prime Minister Menachem Begin, who had never apologized to him for mocking Yiddish. Israel had no budget for supporting the learning of Yiddish. The state had gotten its priorities wrong, he deplored.

"For hundreds of years, Jews spoke Yiddish. And today, a

splendid literary tradition is going down the drain. To claim that the history of the Jewish people started with Chaim Weizmann is a serious mistake. I can't understand why Israel despises Yiddish, spits on it. Yiddish is a language that accompanied the Jews to the ghettos, the ovens, everywhere. Why don't Israelis study Yiddish in the Hebrew schools, in the teachers' colleges, the universities, in the same manner they study English, French, and Hebrew? Isn't Yiddish part of our culture? Our fathers and our forefathers? Why be ashamed of them? With our own hands, we educate our children against us!" He was almost shouting. His blue eyes flashed with rage, and his whole body trembled. This emotional outburst triggered an attack of coughing. And again Alma begged him to stop talking, but without much success. My father could not be silenced. These were words of harsh, penetrating rebuke, and I sensed that they might perhaps be his last vigorous reprimand. I can still hear each word.

The next time I would see him, Alzheimer's would have begun to gnaw at his brain, and he would barely recognize me. This dinner was to be one of his last good times. In the throes of his passion, he seemed to have forgotten his pain, and like a furious prophet, he raged against his people, his Jewish brothers, whom he denounced as being the real mortal enemy of Judaism.

We left the restaurant. Alma held my father by one arm and I held the other. She implored me not to talk to him. Walking was already a great effort that demanded most of his physical strength. We walked in silence for some time. Now and then someone would point at him and whisper. His picture had often appeared in the newspapers lately, since his literary agents had seen to it that his hitherto neglected works were all back in print.

As we approached the gate of my father's building, an

attractive young woman walked past us. My father stopped and turned his head with an admiring look on his face.

"Still?" I asked incredulously.

"As long as there's breath in my body," he replied with his old, charming smile. "I may be a bit deaf and blind and even a little senile, but I still notice a pretty face."

He was no penitent.

27

WHEN YOUR BRAIN BETRAYS YOU

I wanted to see my father one last time. From Alma's telephone reports, it was clear that his condition was deteriorating rapidly. She warned me that on my next visit I would find a completely different man. "I'm not sure you should see him in his decline, but if you insist, I can't refuse. I'll send you some money." And following his practice, she asked me to buy the cheapest ticket to New York.

I arrived prepared. From my reading about Alzheimer's disease, I had learned that the patient can clearly remember what happened fifty or sixty years ago but has no short-term memory. I naively believed that if I read him passages of his book *Satan in Goray,* which had been written in the late thirties, or chapters of the Bible, which he had studied in his youth, those words and sounds would bring him back to me. Alma had told me that sometimes he was lucid for a little while, and I hoped that I would somehow succeed in extending those moments of lucidity.

Miami Beach, August 1990: Despite having been prepared for the normal Miami summer of blazing, tropical weather, I was overwhelmed by the stifling and exhausting combination of heat and humidity that welcomed me. The newspapers were full of the impending war in the Persian Gulf.

The doorman of their apartment building greeted me: "Mrs. Singer asked me to tell you that they're having lunch at Danny's," he said, and gave me directions to get there. "You can't miss it," he said. I hurried over. I could see in the distance the colorful sign listing various Jewish delicacies: knishes, kishke, matzo balls, and *cholent*. Dozens of old men escorted by black or Hispanic nurses were eating. I recognized my father from his bald head and light-skinned face gleaming in the distance. He was sitting in a wheelchair across from Alma, and next to him was his nurse, Mrs. Amporo, whom I knew from telephone conversations. What I saw shocked me. I saw an old man with a drooping face gaping at me with no expression. I came up and kissed him. He looked surprised at me.

"Who's this guy who's bothering me?" he asked Alma.

"It's me, Israel, your son," I replied. "You remember me, don't you?"

His face remained expressionless. Alma had warned me on the phone that he might not recognize me. It was the nurse's turn to try her hand: "Mr. Singer, your son came from Israel to see you." But her words too fell on deaf ears. How he had aged. His face was shriveled and withered, his body looked weak and frail, and his hands shook. His legs could no longer hold him up, and he no longer ate on his own; the nurse fed him like a baby. I was frozen as if dumbstruck. I couldn't take my eyes off him.

"I'm your son, Gigi, from Warsaw, from 57 Leszno Street." I said the number in Polish, hoping against all hope that he'd remember.

Then, all of a sudden, he blinked his eyes, raised his eyebrows, and said: "Oh, you're my son, Gigi? You came to see me? I'm very glad you came."

I kissed his cold hand and began telling him stories about his grandchildren and his great-grandson Avichai. He looked at the picture of the baby and said it was himself in a previous incarnation. While I was giving him regards from my wife, he turned to Alma and asked with a blank look: "Who is this man who doesn't stop talking to me?" The connection had been cut off. His face went completely blank. There were a few brief moments of recognition, but most of the time he regarded me as a stranger. The disease had devastated him. His extraordinary memory had been wiped out altogether. The nurse went on feeding him. In the middle of the meal he closed his eyes and fell sound asleep, his lips smacking and twitching uncontrollably.

"That's how he is most of the time," sighed Alma.

All my efforts to rouse him and bring him back to me failed. I tried everything to reach him, to preserve in my memory one more conversation with him, one more happy smile — in vain. I had been warned, Alma reminded me.

We left the restaurant and headed home. The nurse pushed the wheelchair with the sleeping old man, his head drooping on his shoulder. Collins Avenue was full of old people like him. A heavyset black woman was taking an old man to Sheldon's Drugstore, and to my surprise, she was speaking to him in Yiddish: "Sam, just a little more and we're there." We returned to my father's apartment building, where the doorman helped bring the wheelchair inside.

Most mornings, my father sat dozing in the wheelchair by the swimming pool. A few women his age, still wearing bikinis, swam in the pool. Their skin was wrinkled and shriveled. I couldn't recall ever seeing old women in bikinis on the beach in Tel Aviv. But Miami Beach was different. It was one big old people's colony — as if all the Elders of Zion had convened here for a conference on aging.

I was advised by Alma to visit my father twice a day, in the morning at the swimming pool and in the afternoon in the lobby of his apartment building. There was a television set in the lobby, and my father and other very senior citizens watched it dully, clearly comprehending neither sights nor sounds. He mostly dozed. I looked at him and couldn't understand how a person who was once so alert and active could sit all day and gaze blankly. When my father was awake, he was often very short-tempered. Something always seemed to be bothering him, and no one could help him. I couldn't take my eyes off him. He was dressed neatly, in a clean shirt, pressed trousers, and matching tie. He was obviously well cared for, washed, clean; everything was fine, except that his brain had betrayed his body. Once, during one of those visits, out of nowhere — perhaps some inner vision — he shouted very loudly: "Naamah!"

None of us knew who Naamah was. I rummaged around in my memory for a long time. Had there been a Naamah among his many lady friends? He hadn't told me about her. I tried recalling the characters in all his works, and I finally remembered the demon Naamah from "The Death of Methuselah," the unforgettable lover of the 969-year-old Methuselah, who came to take him to the city Cain had built, where "lechery is no sin," as he had written in his story. Was it really her he missed? Could it be that he had dealings with King Asiel, "whose semen filled [her] womb?"

None of my attempts to read him passages from *Satan in Goray* roused him from his torpor, and the Bible had no effect either. Then later, as I was sitting one day with him, he suddenly sighed and blurted out: "We're so poor. The publishers robbed us of everything."

Alma explained to me that in recent years he had been obsessed with the feeling that he had been robbed and would wind up destitute. I told her that during my last visit, my father had asked if I would translate two of his books into Hebrew for nothing because he didn't have a cent to pay me. I had already translated all his books for free and would be glad to go on doing it, I answered him. "Don't worry, I'll pay you," he had repeated several times.

I was moved by and appreciated the way Alma took care of my father. I admired her all the more knowing how frustrating and difficult it is to be with such a sick person twenty-four hours a day. She repeatedly assured me that she would never put him in a nursing home where the patients are ignored. When he was near death, she finally gave in and took him to a geriatric hospital. But she sat at his bed day and night with two nurses all the time he was there.

I visited him only a few hours a day. Most of my time was spent walking idly around Collins Avenue and getting to know that depressing city of old Jewish people. According to various estimates, there are about thirty thousand elderly citizens in Miami. The geriatric care they receive, I was told, is as good as one can get. All city services are aimed at easing the end of their lives and giving them pleasure.

At the counter of Sheldon's Drugstore, I met a man in his late eighties who told me that he knew my father well and had read most of his books. In earlier years, when my father had been healthy, the two of them would tell each other stories. "Today your father's kaput. They won't even take him at the club." They've got a club with everything anybody could possibly want, he said with a Yiddish accent, even a marriage counselor. My father knew her. A charming woman. Most of them were already "post-sex," but nevertheless it was hard to be alone. The counselor, the man told me, a psychologist, believed that two people were better than one alone at any age. He told me that my father used to question her and listen to her many tales. I knew that some of my father's stories had gotten their inspiration from and were written about the old people of that club, most of them widows or widowers. As for my elderly friend, he had lived here twelve years and had already gone through six wives. "Six wives in twelve years?" I said with admiration.

He laughed. "When you raise your eyebrows, you remind me so much of your father, same blue eyes and same chin. Here you don't get married," he explained. "Here, everybody keeps his own money. The main thing is to be together, but everyone pays his own expenses separately, down to the last cent. It's not easy to tie up with an old woman and split everything with her. What if it doesn't work out? The children generally aren't happy about it either; they're afraid they'll inherit less."

The counselor maintained to all who would listen that it was important to have somebody, aside from a nurse. The nurse might even steal from you and is always hinting that you shouldn't forget her in your will. "You see, it's nicer to end the story with two."

I asked my Casanova about his six wives. The matches were experimental, he explained. After a while, you had a discussion with the counselor and, if necessary, put an end to the test. "Your father loved to listen to the stories."

"But six wives in such a short time?" I asked.

"I see that the apple doesn't fall far from the tree, as they say. So you want to know everything, eh?"

The first wife apparently snored so loud that he couldn't sleep, even though they had separate rooms. The second one never shut up and chattered constantly. The third one had a nervous breakdown and had to be hospitalized. The fourth one committed suicide by jumping out the window. ("Your father mentioned her in one of his stories.") The fifth one cheated on him with the man next door! They were on the phone to each other all the time. Now he was with Bayla, a good woman. The counselor said that it was a match made in heaven.

"How do you meet people here?" I wondered. I remembered reading in one of my father's stories that many of the retired people who live in Florida are thoroughly absorbed in the stock market. For meeting people, there are apparently a great many social activities such as bingo, bridge, exercises, dancing, lectures, and personal discussions with the counselor.

"Everybody here is looking for a little bit of love," explained my informant, who pulled a round tin box from his pocket and swallowed about half a dozen pills of various colors.

Since many of these old people have trouble walking, a bank representative usually comes to their apartments twice a week and arranges their accounts, including their stock market investments. Similarly, twice a week, a lady from a big clothing store visits many of the ladies at home, bringing along a selection of clothes — an enormous rack of expensive, fashionable dresses. His sixth wife-partner, Bayla, he told me, would closet herself in with the saleswoman in the apartment and try on all the garments while the Yiddish-speaking saleswoman made sure that the dresses fit properly. These women buy the most expensive clothes. "Bayla's closet, for instance, is bursting at the seams. What do I care? It's her money, and she says she doesn't want to take it with her. Come to our club some Friday night, Israel, and you'll see a fashion show they wouldn't be ashamed to show in Paris, London, or Tel Aviv."

A few days later, my daughter Merav, who was studying clinical psychology at Stanford University, came to Miami Beach, and together we paid a visit to my father. Unfortunately, even that pretty young woman couldn't arouse him. She devoted most of her time to Alma, who seemed delighted to be with a young woman for a change. They went shopping together.

The subject of inheritance had never come up. My father refused to talk about it. He apparently didn't believe that the day would ever come when he too would have to meet his maker. I wonder whether he felt that writing about life after death had exempted him from dying. Alma was astonished that I had never talked about any of this with him when he was healthy. "I tried, but didn't succeed," I told her.

At night, I would help her change my father's wet sheets. He refused to get out of bed, and we had to shift him around while he fought us desperately and clung to the bed frame with all his might. I barely succeeded in lifting him while Alma spread a clean sheet beneath him. I admired once again her extraordinary devotion, especially since she wasn't all that much younger than my father.

In late August 1990, with the Persian Gulf War threatening to erupt in the Middle East, I had to leave my father to return to Israel. I kissed him good-bye and he remained expressionless, absent, perhaps even alienated, steeped in his own world. I kept glancing at the 1978 winner of the Nobel Prize for literature, who had written an entire opus and shaken the hands of kings and dukes twelve years ago. There was my father — removed from the world, from thinking, from writing — sitting like a broken vessel in a wheelchair.

Eleven months later, his suffering came mercifully to an end.

28

I LEARNED TO LOVE HIM

My father didn't believe that he too would die one day. He had plumbed the depths of the subject and had come to the conclusion that the body may be destroyed, but the soul would wander around in the world forever. Apparently he didn't fear the day of his death because, in his fertile imagination, he had already been through various incarnations. Once he pointed to a pigeon with a fringe of black feathers on his head and decided that the soul of a rabbi was hidden inside the bird. He firmly rejected death as the final end. At the age of eighty-two, he was still making abundant plans: he was preparing to write a play that would take Broadway by storm, he claimed, a popular children's book about the chronicles of philosophy throughout the world, and a novel about the Jews of the Khazar kingdom.

When I visited him in the last year his mind was still clear, he suggested, as usual, that we go to the "attic" — the room filled with papers, books, newspapers, manuscripts, and magazines all heaped up at random on the floor. Whenever he came across an article or a book that he thought might help him in his writing, he would store it in that room. It was also stacked high with dozens of translations of his books in various languages, books with emotional dedications that had been sent to him by writers and poets, certificates of literary prizes, medals, honorary doctorates — it was all there. We loved to spend time together in that room, talking as our hands picked among the newspapers and books. Each time we pulled an old book or manuscript out of a pile, a new anecdote would pop up.

My father told me that one day, while he was searching at the bottom of a pile, his fingers came on a cardboard box. What's a box doing here? he wondered, and with great effort, he managed to pull it out. When he opened the moldy cardboard box, he got very excited. In it were some sixty short stories and three unfinished novels. He gazed at the treasure and shouted with excitement: "Oh, my God, I've got to live another hundred years to edit the stories, translate them into English, and publish them!"

He had written some of the material in the early fifties, he remembered, but a pipe had burst in the room where he kept his papers, and the room had flooded with water. He had been convinced that the material was lost. When he discovered the treasure, he rushed to call his secretary, Dvora Menashe. They both began sorting it out, editing, and translating. Some of the stories were published during his lifetime. According to his friend and publisher Roger Straus, the work was left incomplete, and it will probably provide copious subjects for future doctoral dissertations.

I was often asked whether we ever managed to bridge the gap of our twenty-year separation. The lapse of years was certainly discernible on an emotional level. I didn't miss him very much when we were apart, as I missed my own children when I was out of Israel. But a deep friendship between us was created — tightened as a result of working together on translations and engaging in long conversations in New York and Israel. As for his relations with my mother, although in the beginning I listened to both sides, I made a point of systematically refusing to take sides with either of them.

During a radio interview, I was asked whether I thought that my father had loved me. It was a tricky question, and I had a hard time answering it. Throughout my life, I don't recall hearing any words of affection from him. He regarded expressions of feeling as melodrama, and we never touched on emotions. His love was reserved for the women in his life. And so what Isaac Bashevis Singer actually felt for his son remains a riddle to me. He was comfortable with me, I felt, and he never hesitated to tell me his deep, private secrets. He was sincerely pleased when I came to America. He also hoped that I would bring along a new Hebrew translation. It was clear from the start that it was almost unnatural for him to act like an ordinary grandfather to his grandchildren. When my daughter traveled to New York with her husband and called to tell him that she was about to visit him for the first time, he quickly summoned my friend Natan Shaham, the writer, to join them, "at least for the first hour," because he didn't know how to talk with "children."

I recently came across an article my father published in *The Forward* titled "From the Old and New House," dating from the time he started writing his memoirs. He began the article by explaining that he had made a mistake in the structure of his memoirs. And what was that mistake? He had forgotten to tell his readers about his son. He was now correcting that omission:

> I made a mistake in the structure of these memoirs, and I can't go on writing until I correct it. I forgot to talk about one of the most important events in my life.

In early 1955, I received a letter from my son in
Israel. In previous chapters, I have already told that
after my son's mother was expelled from Soviet
Russia to Turkey, she managed to escape to Palestine.
That was, I think, in 1938. In Palestine she lived on
Kibbutz Beit-Alfa for a long time, and Gigi (his name
is Israel) was educated there. When the war broke out
between Israel and the Arabs, Israel went into the
army. From time to time, I received messages from
him. My colleague at *The Forward,* Hone Gutesfeld,
who was one of the first American writers to visit the
state of Israel right after the war, brought me regards
from my son, who had traveled to Gutesfeld in his
army clothes to inquire about me.

I hadn't seen my son Israel since my arrival in
America some twenty years back. The baby I had left
in Warsaw had grown up without me. Now here was
this letter in which Israel wrote to me of his planned
visit to America.

In a story titled "The Son," which was published
in Yiddish in *Die Goldene Keyt,* in English in the
Menorah, and in Hebrew in *Me'oznaim,* I described
that visit years later. The story is about that one night
when I went to meet my son, whom I really didn't
know and who was arriving in New York on an
Israeli ship. There was a great deal of turmoil on that
ship: everything was new and unusual: the fact that
the Jews had a country, that a ship sailed the sea with
a blue and white flag. Jews were dancing, laughing,
shouting. The officers spoke Hebrew, which
sounded to me like Italian or Spanish from the distance. The ship was late, and when it finally did

come, it took several hours until all the passengers were off. Israel was the last one to disembark. I was nervous, and perhaps even afraid of that encounter, since I had never had any experience in fatherhood; but natural relations of father and son were created between us straightaway. Israel isn't tall, but he's a healthy fellow with blond hair and blue eyes. Back in Israel, on the kibbutz, he devoted a lot of time to breeding fish in a "pond." Today he's a teacher in the high school at Beit-Alfa, but in those days, he was a fisherman. For a fisherman, he was very intelligent. He played chess and occasionally published a chess problem. During his lifetime, he had spoken Yiddish, Polish, Russian, and even Turkish; but he had forgotten all those languages and knew only Hebrew. Along with all the other apprehensions and fears, I was afraid I wouldn't be able to talk to my son in my old-fashioned version of the Holy Tongue.

Everything turned out better than I thought. We managed to communicate well and even held long conversations. Louise [i.e., Alma] was fond of him and treated him like a mother. That son of mine turned out wonderfully independent and sensitive. On the very first day, he took the subway and went to visit some people in Brooklyn, despite the fact that he didn't know how to get there. He looked at a map and made up his mind to travel to California. Instead of asking me for money, he published an ad to drive a car or truck to California. He had an international driver's license. Soon after he came, he drove a car by himself to Los Angeles. To someone like me who had ridden a bench in a prayer house, such a skill seemed

unbelievable. But Israel belonged to the new generation. He was a sergeant in the Israeli army, knew how
to shoot, swim, drive a truck or a tractor, and ride
horses. His temperament was good, and he was not at
all impetuous or nervous, a perfect gentleman. I
immediately learned to love him. He showed the
same feelings for me.

For a time he lived with me. But later on, he
moved. He had a lot of friends, and was a representative of the kibbutz or the party in all kinds of assem-
blies. They invited him to Hebrew camps. I soon
realized that he was not going to bother me.

Israel told me that he had a girl on the kibbutz
whom he would bring to America for a few months,
but it was hard to get permission from the army. A lot
of letters from her came to my address. So, here I had
been childless for many years, and now I was about to
marry off my son and become a father-in-law. I was
half-serious and half-mocking about the whole
thing, as I am about all such things. I was happy my
son suited my taste; for if he had been a bad, cheating,
gluttonous, bitter man, the fact that I was his father
wouldn't have helped him. During the few months
we were together, he told me about his life. The war
years had been one big nightmare. He told me of his
countless dangers. I also learned about all his girls.
Despite all the bright and dark sides of life, he remained a solid person. In my opinion, he lacked only
one thing: ambition. He was willing to spend his life
as a fisherman on a kibbutz. I later discovered from
some of the articles he showed me that he was a
rather talented writer. He didn't plan to become a

professional author. He was the perfect product of
the kibbutz.

In the course of his visit, I had to take a long trip.
Israel remained in America, and naturally I gave him
the keys to my apartment.

My father's memories were inaccurate. I had asked him for
the keys to his apartment, and he had categorically refused. The
selectivity of his memory is interesting. I remember his alienation from me during the early period of our New York reunion,
the fact that he didn't give me any financial assistance, and that
it was only after I started working and earning some money that
he "adopted" me. He was impressed by the meaningless fact
that I was able to drive a car to Los Angeles.

At any rate, for me, these memories of his, which didn't get
into his memoirs, are like a document that opens only a thin
crack into his feelings. In that article, my father explained
himself in detail to his son: "I immediately learned to love him
for his good qualities." Can that be regarded as a declaration of
love? When he was corresponding with my mother, in the first
years after our immigration to Palestine, he would shower
words of love on me. He even sent me a violin and a bicycle
once. But after the 1948 war, he stopped all contact. I grew up
without him. Memories of my father faded more each year;
they died within me. Over the twenty years that followed, so
did my love for him. When I arrived in New York on my first
visit, I was seeking to close a circle of life. My first trip to see
him derived more from curiosity than from any feelings of love
for an unknown father.

Despite the feelings he professed for me, he often hurt me. In
1980, after publishing a collection of my own stories in
Hebrew, *Horse Shoe,* in Israel, I came to New York and

excitedly handed him the book. He'd be happy, I thought, maybe even proud of his son. He glanced at it for only a few seconds, then he gave it back to me with an angry expression: "Why don't you translate my books instead of writing your own?" His words were like a bucket of ice water poured on my head. I shook with fury and bit my lips.

Back in 1975, I phoned my father to tell him that I had had a son named Yuval. His answer was: "I'm glad about every baby you have. In my lectures I talk a lot about your children. America loves a writer with a big family. It makes for more closeness between the writer and his readers." Everything, no matter what, was always turned toward him. My father was the center of the world and was unable to emote in any normal family way.

In point of fact, he barely knew my children. My father met my daughter Merav when she was five and my son Noam when he was two. He saw Merav twice more, once in New York and once in Miami Beach. He met my third son Ilan on his visit to Israel, but he never saw Yuval, who was born in 1975. When he visited Haifa, I pleaded with him to come to the kibbutz to see my children. He always begged off with the excuse that he wasn't a "family man." America may love a writer with a big family, but my father did not.

After I finished translating *Enemies, a Love Story*, he read every word of it, and said: "I'm very satisfied with the translation. You seem to have secretly plumbed the depths of my intentions and found the right words in Hebrew."

"I'm glad to hear a good word from you."

"Didn't I ever tell you that?"

"No."

"Well, I'll tell you more than that, I'm glad I've got a son like you and not a daughter."

I didn't quite understand this statement, and he never elaborated or explained it to me. Why would he prefer a son to a daughter? Recently, the theater director of HaBima, Hanan Snir, told me that when he worked with my father on *Yentl* in Switzerland, my father kept asking him why he wasn't married. A year later, when they met again, Hanan was married. My father asked him if he had a son or a daughter and if he thought it made a difference. Hanan replied that he didn't care one way or another. "I never wanted a daughter," my father remarked, without being prompted.

Somewhat shocked, Hanan asked my father for an explanation.

"I wouldn't want men to do to my daughter all the things I've done to women," he replied.

On that subject, he wrote to my mother in 1938:

> And now to dear Gigi. I kiss him a thousand times and think about him and love him. I hope I'll be able to play with him as he and I loved to do. I don't have and won't have any children except for Gigi. When I work and earn money, I'll give him whatever he wants. I hope he'll have a chance to study and grow up to be a healthy, happy fellow. I dread only one thing: that he should make me a grandfather — I've got no desire for that at all.

Despite distance, hearts manage to make contact in their own twisted and complicated way. And in that way, we made peace with one another. When I stood at my father's grave in Beth-El Cemetery, holding the shovel in my hands and covering his coffin with earth, I knew that I was burying only his body; my father's soul — his literary legacy — lives on. Generations to come will be enriched and entertained by his works. They will read and appreciate him as an exciting, fascinating writer. As I started my journey to my father, I rebelled against him, his works, his worldview, his Diaspora life, his superstitions, his belief in demons and ghosts. Our opinions were often divided on many subjects, but over the years we grew closer together. His religious and mystical beliefs are still alien to me. I have matured politically and have recovered from the blind Stalinist education I received in my youth. The Soviet Union, that "fortress of progress," has sunk, and I have moved far away from the dogmas I grew up on. We both found the proper balance between the emotional dilemmas of a son who set out to know his father and a father who didn't know what a son was or how to behave with him. A complicated journey it was for both of us. I came to know his life, his past, and our rich and lush Jewish culture, whose aromas intoxicate me. Perhaps all that in its own way helped me make up for lost time.

The day after my father's funeral, my wife Aviva and I decided to go to Ellis Island, the so-called Island of Tears, and visit the entrance to America. As we passed by Lady Liberty, she seemed to be waving at us. A chill wind blew from the sea. Ellis Island had changed. It is now an immigration museum, honoring millions of immigrants from all over the world. Faces of hardworking Jewish immigrants from the shtetl were looking at us from one of the walls. My father had devoted his life to them. He spoke on behalf of those Jews, with packs on their backs and fear on their faces as they saw the land before them and fretted that they might not be allowed in. I looked at those faces a long time, and for a moment I imagined my father's presence among them. An unexpected tear came to my eye. In this Ellis Island pilgrimage, I had returned to my father in a kind of private funeral. I was adding yet another tear to the Island of Tears.